How to Read People Like a Book

Master Social Cues, Body Language and Facial Expressions; the Power of Non-Verbal Communication in Decoding Human Behavior

Erica May

any other individual or persons for any purpose other than that for which it was initially intended. It is strictly prohibited to amend, reproduce, distribute, utilize, quote, or paraphrase any part of the content within this publication without prior authorization from the writer or publisher. Any violation of these regulations may result in legal action against those who have breached them.

Disclaimer Notice

The presented work is strictly informational and should not be interpreted as an offer to buy or sell any form of security, instrument, or investment vehicle. Furthermore, the information contained herein should not be taken as a medical, legal, tax, accounting, or investment recommendation given by the author(s) or any affiliated company, employees, or paid contributors. In other words, the information is presented without considering individual preferences for specific investments regarding risk parameters. General information does not account for a person's lifestyle and financial objectives. It is important to note that no tailored advice will be provided based on the given information.

Table of Contents

CHAPTER 3: CRACKING THE CODE: THE SCIENCE OF NONVERBAL CUES

Welcome to the

Ideas Worth Sharing

Series

My name is Nicholas Bright, and I've spent nearly two decades working as a psychologist specializing in Behavioral Neuroscience and Interpersonal Communication in the US, UK, and Australia. Throughout my career, I've encountered countless stories, experiences, and insights that have shaped my understanding of the human mind and interpersonal interactions.

This series is a collaborative effort, bringing together the experience and expertise of myself and my colleagues: Erica May, Jeff Sharpe, Camila Alvarez, and potentially new faces in the future! We've chosen to write under pen names to respect everyone's privacy and keep the spotlight on the valuable content we offer rather than us as individuals. This decision allows us to freely share our knowledge without the distractions that often come with the limelight. We stand by the authenticity and credibility of the content shared here—our professional integrity remains at the forefront of this series.

We are deeply passionate about our field, and our primary goal is to equip you with practical, research-backed insights that you can implement in your everyday life. Each chapter is designed to inspire and help you better understand yourself and those around you.

We invite you to engage actively with the material: take notes, discuss the ideas with friends and family, and, most importantly, apply the lessons in your daily routine.

1. **Read;** understand what can be done to improve
2. **Reflect;** appreciate your feelings and their origins
3. **Remember;** put your learning into action

Thank you for embarking on this journey of knowledge and growth with us,

Nick

Want to Win Free Books?

Join Our Newsletter!

In this series, we appreciate that someone may find many different books helpful. I certainly know that when discussing sensitive topics like, for example, divorce, we can end up working on grief, anxiety, self-confidence, cognitive dissonance, and lots more. When we encounter a major challenge in life, it is rarely due to one small problem but rather a concoction of our experiences, outlooks, and actions; it's often a deep-rooted issue with many different things we need to uncover and support. We are complicated beings, and we must recognize this. As such, I would love to invite you all to join our newsletter.

In this, I aim to write articles of interest, including excerpts from various books in the series, as well as **vouchers**, **discounts**, and **giveaways**—and of course, no gimmicks or catches. I harbor a deep loathing of companies that offer seemingly amazing deals, only to charge you vast amounts in hidden fees! I vowed to never fall into that trap myself, and any offers I make are designed to be of true benefit and help. If you win a book in a giveaway, I want you to read it with a smile.

Join our newsletter and discover the additional value we can add to your life's curriculum!

Join us at: **www.IdeasWorthSharingSeries.com/newsletter**

See you on the inside!

About the Author: Dr. Erica May

Dr Erica May is a dedicated Clinical Psychologist practising in New York City. She graduated from Syracuse University in New York State, earning her degree in Clinical Psychology. Erica specializes in Cognitive Behavioral Therapy (CBT), Dialectical Behavior Therapy (DBT), and trauma-focused treatments. Her work is deeply rooted in helping individuals navigate complex emotional landscapes, enabling them to lead healthier and more fulfilling lives. Her compassionate approach and expertise have garnered her a reputation as a trusted mental health professional in her local community.

Erica has been friends and has worked with Nicholas Bright, the lead author of the Ideas Worth Sharing series, for many years. Together, they aim to help support a wider community by writing a book series on important topics within Psychology and extending their therapeutic insights and techniques beyond the confines of their practice. This book series will cover various topics related to mental health, including detailed guides on implementing CBT and DBT strategies in daily life, as well as comprehensive approaches to prevention, understanding and healing. By presenting practical exercises and learning through her practice, Erica hopes to make evidence-based psychological concepts more accessible to a broader audience. She aims to empower individuals with the knowledge and tools to manage their mental health proactively and independently, fostering greater resilience and well-being.

Preface

"The most important thing in communication

is hearing what isn't said."

Peter Drucker

In this book, we embark on a journey to explore the often-overlooked but immensely powerful world of nonverbal communication and emotional intelligence. I aim to provide you with a comprehensive guide that enlightens the subtle intricacies of human behavior and equips you with the skills to interpret these cues effectively. Whether in professional settings or personal interactions, mastering this silent language can profoundly transform your understanding of others and enhance your interpersonal relationships.

The inspiration for this book stemmed from observing the struggles many face in reading and interpreting unspoken signals during interactions. As time passed, I noticed a recurring theme: brilliant individuals fail to make an impact due to their inability to perceive or express nonverbal cues effectively.

Determined to bridge this gap, I sought insights from various psychology, sociology, and behavioral science experts. Alongside these academic pillars, the real-life experiences shared by numerous workshop participants have been invaluable. Their stories have not only enriched this book but have also reinforced the necessity of its creation.

I extend my deepest gratitude to everyone who shared their journey with me, providing both inspiration and real-world validation of the strategies discussed herein. Special thanks go to my mentor, Dr. Emily Tran, whose relentless support and insightful feedback were pivotal throughout the writing process.

This book is designed for those eager to enhance their interpersonal skills and emotional intelligence—managers, sales professionals, customer service representatives, or anyone looking to improve personal relationships. It assumes no prior expertise in psychology or related fields, making it accessible to anyone interested in better understanding human behavior.

By engaging with this content, you are taking a significant step towards becoming more adept at navigating complex social landscapes. The practical exercises will help you apply these insights immediately, fostering personal growth and improving your interactions with others.

Thank you for choosing to invest your time with this guide. As you turn each page, I invite you to delve deeper into human emotions and behaviors, unlocking new levels of empathy and effectiveness in your communication. Let's decode the silent language and discover how much can be heard in what isn't said.

Introduction

"Effective communication is 20% what you know

and 80% of how you feel about

what you know."

Jim Rohn

Understanding and mastering nonverbal communication is a crucial skill that transcends words, weaving subtle yet profound connections between people. In a world where messages constantly cross borders and cultures, the ability to interpret unspoken signals has never been more important. This book delves into the core of nonverbal communication, equipping you with the knowledge to navigate the complexities of human interaction with empathy and insight.

Throughout these pages, you will embark on a journey to decode the silent language we use, often without realizing it. From the tilt of a head to the shifting of feet, nonverbal cues convey a wealth of information that can enhance or undermine verbal communication. By becoming more attuned to these cues, you can better understand the people around you, fostering trust and connection.

One of the key themes explored is cultural sensitivity. Nonverbal communication varies significantly across cultures, and what is considered polite or respectful in one society might be interpreted differently in another. Understanding these cultural nuances is essential for building meaningful relationships in an increasingly interconnected world. The insights will help you avoid common pitfalls and confidently navigate cross-cultural interactions.

The book is structured to guide you step by step through the intricate world of nonverbal communication, starting with the basics and gradually introducing more complex concepts. You will learn about the universal and culture-specific aspects of body language, the impact of facial expressions, and the importance of tone and posture. Each chapter builds on the previous one, creating a cohesive and comprehensive guide to reading and interpreting nonverbal signals.

Emotional intelligence also plays a significant role in effective nonverbal communication. By becoming more aware of your emotions and those of others, you can better manage your responses and interactions. This self-awareness is critical in professional settings, allowing you to navigate challenging situations gracefully and empathetically.

Real-world applications of nonverbal communication are emphasized throughout the book. Whether leading a team, negotiating a business deal, or simply engaging in everyday conversations, the skills you will develop are practical and applicable. By integrating these techniques into your daily life, you will find that your interactions become more meaningful and productive.

The importance of continuous learning is another theme that permeates this book. Human behavior is a dynamic and ever-evolving field; there is always more to discover. The tools and strategies provided here are not a one-time solution but a foundation you can build. By staying curious and open-minded, you can continue enhancing your communication skills.

You will also find exercises and practical tips to help you practice and refine your abilities. Consistent effort and mindful observation are key to becoming proficient in nonverbal communication. Starting with small goals, such as noticing the alignment of expressions and spoken words, will set you on the path to mastery.

As you progress through the book, remember that the journey is as important as the destination. Each interaction is an opportunity to learn and grow. Embracing the insights and techniques presented here will improve your communication skills and enrich your relationships and personal development.

In conclusion, this book offers a gateway to understanding a vital aspect of human interaction. Reading and responding to nonverbal cues can transform your communication, allowing you to build stronger connections and navigate various social scenarios more easily. Embrace the journey, and let these pages guide you toward a deeper understanding of the silent language that unites us all.

Chapter 1: The Silent Symphony: Decoding the Language of Nonverbal Communication

"Communication works for those who work at it."

John Powell

Unlocking the Hidden Messages in Everyday Interactions

Nonverbal communication is a powerful yet often overlooked aspect of human interaction. Every day, we engage in countless exchanges where words are merely the tip of the iceberg. Beneath the surface lies a rich tapestry of body language, facial expressions, gestures, and postures that convey our true thoughts and emotions. Understanding these nonverbal cues can transform how we connect with others, enhancing personal and professional relationships.

Nonverbal communication is not just an add-on to verbal exchanges; it is integral to how others perceive and perceive us. Research shows that a significant portion of our communication is nonverbal, making it essential to decode these signals accurately. For instance, a simple smile or frown can speak over a hundred words. By mastering nonverbal communication, you gain an invaluable toolset for navigating social landscapes with greater ease and effectiveness.

Consider how often misunderstandings arise from misinterpreted gestures or facial expressions. A colleague's crossed arms might be read as disinterested when it's merely a sign of being cold. You can avoid such pitfalls by honing your ability to read these subtle cues, fostering clearer and more empathetic interactions. The first step in this journey is recognizing the significance of nonverbal communication in our daily lives.

The Elements of Nonverbal Communication

Nonverbal communication encompasses various elements—body language, facial expressions, gestures, and posture—all contributing to the silent symphony of human interaction. Each component plays a unique role in conveying messages that words alone cannot express. Body language, for example, includes everything from eye contact to how we position our bodies during a conversation. These physical manifestations often reveal our true feelings and intentions.

Facial expressions are another critical element, offering insights into emotions that may be hidden behind spoken words. A fleeting look of surprise or doubt can provide context that verbal communication lacks. Similarly, gestures—conscious hand movements or unconscious fidgeting—add layers of meaning to our interactions. Even something as simple as a nod can signify agreement or understanding without uttering a word.

Understanding these elements allows us to interpret nonverbal cues more accurately, leading to better comprehension and fewer misunderstandings. It also equips us with the skills to project confidence and empathy through nonverbal behaviors.

The Impact on Personal and Professional Success

Mastering nonverbal communication can have profound effects on both personal and professional success. Being attuned to nonverbal signals can deepen connections and foster trust in personal relationships. Imagine discerning when a loved one needs support, even if they haven't explicitly said so. Such sensitivity can strengthen bonds and enhance emotional intimacy.

In professional settings, effective nonverbal communication is equally crucial. It can influence how colleagues perceive you, impacting teamwork and leadership dynamics. For instance, maintaining eye contact during meetings can convey confidence and attentiveness, which are highly valued in any workplace. Conversely, being able to read the room—sensing discomfort or enthusiasm through body language—can guide you in steering conversations more effectively.

The benefits extend beyond immediate interactions and contribute to long-term relationship building. People skilled at interpreting nonverbal cues are often seen as more empathetic and trustworthy, qualities that foster lasting connections, whether in business or personal life.

Practical Steps for Mastery

To harness the power of nonverbal communication effectively, start by observing your behaviors and those around you. Notice how people react physically during conversations—their posture, eye movements, and facial expressions. Practice mirroring positive body language in your interactions; this helps build rapport and makes others feel understood.

Engage in active listening by focusing not just on words but also on accompanying gestures and expressions. This holistic approach will enable you to respond more empathetically and appropriately. Regularly reflect on your interactions; consider what worked well and where misinterpretations occurred due to overlooked nonverbal cues.

Incorporating these practices into your daily routine will gradually enhance your ability to effectively decode the silent language of human behavior. As you become more adept at interpreting these signals, you'll navigate social situations more confidently and successfully.

A Roadmap for Continued Learning

This chapter introduces the vast world of nonverbal communication—a foundational step toward unlocking deeper insights into human behavior throughout this book. Subsequent chapters will delve into specific aspects such as decoding facial expressions in various contexts, understanding cultural differences in body language, and applying these skills in specialized settings like negotiations or conflict resolution.

You'll embark on a transformative journey toward heightened emotional intelligence and improved interpersonal relationships by mastering these skills over the coming weeks or months without struggling for practical guidance.

Remember: the key lies in understanding these concepts intellectually and applying them actively in everyday interactions. Each step in understanding this unspoken language will enhance your connections, empathy, and success in every aspect of your life.

Nonverbal communication is the silent symphony that plays a crucial role in our daily interactions, often speaking louder than words. Understanding the significance of nonverbal cues in daily interactions and their influence on relationships is key to fostering better connections with others. While verbal communication conveys the content of our message, nonverbal cues reveal the emotions behind those words, providing valuable insights into a person's true feelings and intentions. Mastering the art of decoding nonverbal signals can greatly enhance one's ability to navigate social situations effectively.

Body language, facial expressions, gestures, and posture are all essential elements of nonverbal communication that convey messages beyond what is spoken. How someone stands, facial expressions and even subtle gestures can communicate volumes about their emotional state and attitude toward others. Paying attention to these nonverbal cues can significantly improve our ability to understand and connect with people on a deeper level.

Nonverbal communication is vital in building trust, empathy, and rapport in personal relationships. When we are attuned to the nonverbal signals of our loved ones, we can better respond to their needs and emotions, fostering stronger bonds and healthier connections. Similarly, mastering nonverbal cues in professional settings can enhance leadership skills, negotiation tactics, and overall communication effectiveness with colleagues and clients.

Recognizing the impact of mastering nonverbal cues on personal and professional success is essential for anyone looking to improve their social interactions. By honing these skills, individuals can become more perceptive communicators, better equipped to navigate the complexities of human behavior with confidence and empathy. The ability to decipher nonverbal signals not only enhances one's emotional intelligence but also paves the way for more authentic and meaningful relationships.

Mastering Nonverbal Communication: The Key to Understanding Beyond Words

Nonverbal communication is a multifaceted language that conveys much information beyond words. Body language, facial expressions, and gestures are essential elements that play a significant role in how we understand and interpret the unspoken messages people convey. Each component provides valuable insights into someone's thoughts, emotions, and intentions, often revealing more than verbal communication alone.

Body language encompasses various cues, including posture, eye contact, and hand movements. A person's posture can speak volumes about their confidence, interest, or discomfort in a given situation. Maintaining open and relaxed body language can signal approachability and receptiveness in social interactions. Eye contact is another crucial aspect of body language that conveys engagement and attentiveness. Being mindful of your body language and observing others' nonverbal cues can lead to more effective communication and deeper connections.

Facial expressions are powerful indicators of emotions and can provide valuable insights into someone's inner state. A smile can signify happiness or friendliness, while furrowed brows may indicate concern or confusion. Understanding the nuances of facial expressions can help you gauge the emotional tone of a conversation and respond appropriately. Paying attention to microexpressions—brief, involuntary facial movements that reveal true emotions—can offer valuable clues about someone's feelings that they may be trying to conceal.

Gestures are another essential component of nonverbal communication that can enhance or detract from your message. Hand gestures can emphasize key points, convey enthusiasm, or clarify verbal communication. However, it's essential to be mindful of cultural differences in gesture meanings to avoid misunderstandings. Using gestures sparingly and purposefully can enhance your communication effectiveness and help you connect with others more authentically.

By honing your awareness of these nonverbal cues, you can become more adept at understanding the unspoken language of human interaction. Recognizing the subtleties of body language, facial expressions, and gestures allows you to communicate more effectively, build stronger relationships, and navigate social situations with confidence and insight. Developing proficiency in decoding nonverbal signals is a valuable skill that can positively impact personal relationships and professional success.

Nonverbal communication is a powerful tool that can significantly impact personal and professional success. Mastering nonverbal cues can enhance relationships, boost emotional intelligence, and improve communication skills. Individuals can navigate social interactions with greater insight and effectiveness by recognizing the subtle signals conveyed through body language, facial expressions, and gestures.

The ability to decode nonverbal cues can lead to more authentic connections with others. Understanding the unspoken messages people convey through posture, eye contact, and hand movements allows for deeper communication beyond words. By honing this skill, individuals can establish rapport, build trust, and foster stronger relationships in both personal and professional settings.

In professional success, mastering nonverbal communication can be a game-changer. Effective nonverbal cues can convey confidence, competence, and credibility, essential traits in leadership roles or during presentations. Being able to interpret the reactions of others in a meeting or negotiation can provide valuable insights into their thoughts and intentions, enabling individuals to respond appropriately and strategically.

Recognizing the impact of mastering nonverbal cues on personal success is equally important. Being attuned to nonverbal signals can deepen emotional connections in personal relationships, such as with friends, family members, or romantic partners. It allows individuals to show empathy, support, and understanding without necessarily verbalizing their feelings, fostering intimacy and trust.

By becoming proficient in decoding nonverbal communication,

individuals can gain a competitive edge in various aspects of their lives. Whether in social gatherings or professional environments, the ability to read body language accurately can provide valuable insights into the emotions and intentions of others. This heightened awareness can lead to more successful interactions, smoother negotiations, and improved communication dynamics.

Mastering nonverbal cues is an ongoing process that requires practice and observation. Individuals can sharpen their skills by paying attention to the subtle nuances of body language and facial expressions in different contexts. Consistent effort in honing this skill will yield significant benefits in personal relationships and professional endeavors, enhancing overall success and fulfillment.

Embracing the significance of nonverbal communication is a key step toward unlocking greater interpersonal effectiveness. By recognizing the impact of mastering these cues on personal and professional success, individuals can take proactive steps toward improving their communication skills and overall quality of life.

Mastering the art of nonverbal communication is not just about deciphering gestures or interpreting facial expressions; it's about truly understanding the unspoken language that governs our interactions and relationships. As explored in this chapter, nonverbal cues are integral to connecting with others, influencing our personal and professional lives profoundly.

By now, you should clearly grasp the significance of nonverbal communication, recognizing how it shapes our daily interactions. The elements such as body language, facial expressions, and gestures are not mere accessories to spoken words but powerful tools that convey emotions and intentions often more accurately than words alone. Understanding these elements can help you navigate social landscapes more easily and confidently.

Moreover, the impact of mastering nonverbal cues cannot be overstated. Whether you're looking to strengthen personal relationships or aiming for professional success, the ability to read and respond to these silent signals can set you apart. Imagine being able to sense unspoken concerns in a meeting or picking up on a friend's discomfort without them having to say a word. These skills are within your reach and can transform your interactions with the world.

Embrace the Journey Ahead

This chapter is just the beginning of an exciting journey into the depths of human behavior. As you continue through this book, you'll uncover more strategies and insights that will empower you to interpret and utilize nonverbal communication effectively. *The benefits awaiting you are immense*: enhanced emotional intelligence, improved relationships, and a more intuitive understanding of those around you.

Remember, this journey is about taking control of your interactions and harnessing the power of nonverbal communication to your advantage. You already possess the innate ability to master these skills; this book will guide you step-by-step towards that mastery.

Stay engaged, practice what you've learned, and look forward to each chapter as another opportunity to unlock new secrets of human behavior. Your commitment to understanding this silent language will yield remarkable results in your personal and professional spheres.

Let's move forward together, confident that every small improvement in your nonverbal communication skills brings you closer to becoming a master interpreter of human behavior. The adventure has just begun—embrace it with enthusiasm!

Chapter 2: The Emotional Intelligence Quotient: Beyond IQ

"To listen well is as powerful a means of

communication and influence

as to talk well."

John Marshall

Unveiling the Power of Emotional Intelligence: A Key to Human Connection

Emotional intelligence (EI) is more than just a buzzword; it's a critical skill that profoundly impacts our ability to decode nonverbal cues and build meaningful relationships. This chapter delves into the significance of EI, illustrating how it transcends traditional measures of intelligence by enabling us to understand and manage our emotions and those of others. Mastering EI can transform your interactions, making them not only more successful but also more enriching.

Emotional intelligence plays a pivotal role in interpreting the silent language of nonverbal communication. Unlike verbal communication, which is direct and explicit, nonverbal cues often require a nuanced understanding that goes beyond mere words. High EI equips individuals to accurately read facial expressions, body language, and tone of voice, enhancing their capacity for effective communication. This skill is indispensable in personal and professional settings where misunderstandings can lead to conflicts or missed opportunities.

The relationship between emotional intelligence and interpersonal success cannot be overstated. Individuals with high EI are adept at navigating social complexities and fostering strong relationships. They excel at empathizing with others, managing conflicts diplomatically, and inspiring trust. This ability stems from their heightened awareness of emotional dynamics, which allows them to respond appropriately in various situations. Consequently, developing EI is essential for anyone looking to improve their social skills and create lasting connections.

Understanding the components of emotional intelligence is the first step toward enhancing this vital skill. Daniel Goleman identifies five key components: self-awareness, self-regulation, motivation, empathy, and social skills. Each component contributes uniquely to our ability to interpret nonverbal cues accurately. For instance, self-awareness helps us recognize our own emotional responses. At the same time, empathy allows us to tune into the emotions of others. These components form a comprehensive framework for understanding and managing emotions effectively.

Self-awareness involves recognizing your emotions and understanding how they affect your thoughts and behavior. This insight is crucial for interpreting your nonverbal signals accurately and ensuring they align with your intended message. Self-regulation means managing your emotions healthy, such as staying calm under pressure or expressing frustration constructively. Motivation encompasses the drive to achieve goals for personal reasons rather than external rewards, providing resilience in challenging times.

Empathy is understanding others' feelings and perspectives without necessarily agreeing with them. It's a cornerstone of effective communication because it enables you to anticipate how someone might react to what you say or do. Finally, social skills involve managing relationships adeptly by finding common ground, building rapport, and influencing others positively.

Practical strategies can be implemented daily to enhance your emotional intelligence. Journaling can boost self-awareness by helping you track emotional patterns over time. Practicing mindfulness aids self-regulation by keeping you grounded in the present moment rather than being overwhelmed by stress or anxiety. Setting personal goals fosters motivation by giving you something meaningful to strive towards. Active listening promotes empathy by encouraging you to fully focus on the speaker without forming immediate judgments.

Improving emotional intelligence directly impacts nonverbal communication skills as well. Self-awareness helps you recognize when your body language might be sending unintended signals. Empathy allows you to pick up on subtle cues from others that might go unnoticed. By integrating these insights into your interactions, you become more attuned to the silent language that underpins human behavior.

Mastering Emotional Intelligence: A Step-by-Step Process

Step 1: Define Emotional Intelligence

- Understand that emotional intelligence is about recognizing and managing your emotions and those of others.
- Realize its importance in decoding nonverbal cues

effectively.

- Appreciate its critical role in building strong interpersonal relationships.

Step 2: Explore the Components of Emotional Intelligence

- Goleman's five components are self-awareness, self-regulation, motivation, empathy, and social skills.
- Recognize how each component aids in interpreting nonverbal signals.
- Use real-life examples for better comprehension.

Step 3: Strategies for Enhancing Emotional Intelligence

- Journal regularly for increased self-awareness.
- Practice mindfulness exercises for better self-regulation.
- Set personal goals to maintain motivation.
- Engage in active listening exercises to improve empathy.
- Participate in social skill-building activities.

Step 4: Integration of Emotional Intelligence in Nonverbal Communication

- Develop self-awareness to monitor your own nonverbal

cues.

- Use empathy to better understand others' unspoken signals.
- Apply these insights consistently across various interactions.

Step 5: Role-Play and Application

- Engage in role-playing scenarios that mimic real-life situations.
- Reflect on these exercises to identify strengths and areas needing improvement.
- Seek feedback from trusted peers or mentors for further development.

Developing emotional intelligence is about understanding and applying concepts consistently until they become second nature. By following this structured process, you'll be well on your way to mastering the silent language that defines human behavior.

Emotional intelligence is a critical skill that goes beyond traditional measures of intelligence. It involves the ability to recognize, understand, and manage both our own emotions and those of others. This skill plays a vital role in interpreting nonverbal cues accurately, allowing us to navigate social interactions with finesse and empathy. By being attuned to the emotions expressed through body language, facial expressions, and tone of voice, we can deepen our understanding of others and build stronger connections.

Understanding emotional intelligence is not just about

recognizing emotions within oneself; it's also about deciphering the unspoken language of emotions that others convey. Nonverbal cues often speak louder than words, providing valuable insights into a person's feelings and intentions. By honing our emotional intelligence, we can pick up on these subtle signals and respond appropriately, fostering more meaningful and authentic relationships.

Interpreting nonverbal cues accurately requires high emotional intelligence, enabling us to grasp the underlying emotions behind a smile, a frown, or a gesture. By being sensitive to these cues, we can avoid misunderstandings and conflicts, leading to smoother interactions and enhanced communication. Emotional intelligence allows us to go beyond surface-level conversations and delve into the deeper layers of human emotions, fostering genuine connections based on empathy and understanding.

Emotional intelligence is not just a personal attribute; it also plays a crucial role in professional settings. In the workplace, understanding nonverbal cues can help us navigate office dynamics, communicate effectively with colleagues and clients, and build strong professional relationships. By developing our emotional intelligence, we can enhance our leadership skills, negotiation abilities, and overall performance at work.

Beyond IQ: The Power of Emotional Intelligence

Enhancing our emotional intelligence opens up a world of possibilities in both personal and professional realms. It empowers us to connect more deeply with others, resolve conflicts peacefully, and navigate social situations gracefully and confidently. In the next section, we will explore how emotional intelligence influences successful interpersonal interactions and delve into practical strategies for boosting this essential skill set.

Emotional intelligence plays a pivotal role in determining the success of our interpersonal interactions. It serves as the foundation for understanding our emotions and those of others, enabling us to navigate social situations with empathy and clarity. By developing emotional intelligence, individuals can enhance their communication skills, cultivate deeper connections, and foster meaningful relationships. This ability to perceive, comprehend, and manage emotions is crucial in building trust and rapport with others, leading to more harmonious interactions in both personal and professional settings.

One key aspect of emotional intelligence is self-awareness. Being attuned to our emotions allows us to regulate our responses effectively, preventing impulsive reactions that could harm relationships. Self-awareness also enables us to recognize how our emotions influence our behavior and decision-making, leading to more intentional and constructive interactions with others. By understanding our emotional triggers and patterns, we can proactively manage them, fostering smoother communication and stronger connections with those around us.

Empathy is another essential component of emotional intelligence that significantly impacts interpersonal interactions. Empathy involves the ability to understand and share the feelings of others, allowing us to communicate with compassion and sensitivity. When we empathize with others, we validate their emotions and experiences, creating a supportive environment for open and honest communication. This deep understanding fosters trust and mutual respect in relationships, leading to more effective collaboration and conflict resolution.

Effective communication is a cornerstone of successful interpersonal interactions, and emotional intelligence is crucial in enhancing this skill. By honing our emotional intelligence, we can better interpret nonverbal cues such as facial expressions, body language, and tone of voice, leading to a more accurate understanding of others' feelings and intentions. This heightened awareness enables us to respond appropriately in conversations, showing empathy, active listening, and genuine interest in the perspectives of others.

Practical strategies can be implemented to enhance emotional intelligence, improve communication, and elevate one's ability to navigate social interactions effectively. Self-awareness is a fundamental pillar of emotional intelligence. Begin by reflecting on your emotions, reactions, and triggers. Recognizing your emotional patterns allows you to respond more thoughtfully in various situations. Practice mindfulness to stay present and attuned to your feelings without judgment. This awareness can help you regulate your emotions more effectively, improving communication outcomes.

Empathy is another crucial aspect of emotional intelligence that fosters better communication. Put yourself in others' shoes to understand their perspectives and emotions. Active listening is a powerful tool for demonstrating empathy. Engage fully in conversations, focusing on understanding rather than just responding. Reflect on what you've heard to ensure clarity and show that you value the other person's input. Cultivate genuine connections by showing empathy and understanding towards others, building trust and rapport that can enhance communication dynamics significantly.

To further enhance emotional intelligence, develop effective communication skills. Clearly articulate your thoughts and feelings while being mindful of your tone and body language. Practice assertiveness by expressing your needs and boundaries respectfully yet confidently. This helps create a conducive environment for open and honest communication. Conflict resolution skills are also vital in improving interpersonal interactions. Learn to address disagreements constructively, focusing on finding solutions rather than escalating conflicts.

It is essential to prioritize self-care. Nurture yourself physically, emotionally, and mentally to maintain a healthy balance that supports your overall well-being. Adequate rest, exercise, and relaxation contribute to emotional resilience and clarity in communication. Seek feedback from trusted individuals to understand how your emotions and communication style impact others. Constructive feedback can be invaluable in identifying areas for growth and improvement.

Continuous learning is key to refining emotional intelligence over time. Stay curious about human behavior, emotions, and communication dynamics. Read books, attend workshops or seminars, and engage in conversations that expand your knowledge and understanding of interpersonal relationships. Embrace challenges as opportunities for growth, viewing setbacks as valuable lessons that contribute to your emotional maturity.

Incorporating these strategies into your daily life can enhance your emotional intelligence for better communication outcomes. Remember that emotional intelligence is a skill that can be developed with practice and dedication. Embrace the journey of self-discovery and growth as you strive towards more meaningful connections with others based on empathy, self-awareness, and effective communication strategies.

Understanding and enhancing emotional intelligence is not just a theoretical exercise; it's a practical necessity for anyone looking to master nonverbal communication and improve their interpersonal interactions. By recognizing and managing our emotions, as well as understanding the emotions of others, we unlock a deeper level of connection that goes beyond words. This chapter has underscored emotional intelligence's critical role in interpreting nonverbal cues, often the most telling aspects of human interaction.

Moreover, the relationship between high emotional intelligence and successful interpersonal interactions cannot be overstated. Individuals who can accurately read nonverbal signals and respond empathetically are likelier to build trust and rapport. These skills are invaluable in personal relationships and professional settings where effective communication is key to success.

We have also explored actionable strategies to enhance your emotional intelligence. Implementing these strategies can transform your communication skills, making your interactions more meaningful and effective. Whether through active listening, self-reflection, or practicing empathy, each step toward improving your emotional intelligence will yield tangible results.

Remember, developing emotional intelligence is a journey that requires commitment and practice. However, the rewards— stronger relationships, better communication, and an enriched understanding of those around you—are well worth the effort. You have the innate ability to master this skill; it simply takes awareness and dedication.

As you continue through this book, keep these insights in mind. Each subsequent chapter will build on this foundation, providing you with more tools to unlock the secrets of human behavior. Your path to mastering nonverbal communication and emotional intelligence starts here, and every step forward brings you closer to becoming an adept interpreter of the silent language we all speak.

Chapter 3: Cracking the Code: The Science of Nonverbal Cues

"The art of communication is the

language of leadership."

James Humes

Unveiling the Science Behind Nonverbal Communication

Nonverbal communication is often misunderstood as an inherent skill, something we are born with and naturally excel at. However, this belief can lead to missed opportunities to improve our understanding and interpretation of nonverbal cues. Contrary to popular belief, the ability to read nonverbal signals is not an intuitive talent but a learned skill grounded in psychology and behavioral science. This chapter aims to demystify these misconceptions and provide the tools necessary to master the silent language that speaks volumes.

Many assume that some individuals are naturally gifted at interpreting body language, facial expressions, and other nonverbal cues. This assumption can be disheartening for those who struggle with social interactions or lack this 'natural' ability. The truth is, just like any other skill, nonverbal communication can be learned and refined through practice and understanding of its underlying principles.

One of the first steps in mastering nonverbal communication is debunking the myth of innate skillfulness. Research has shown that even professionals who excel in this field have spent years studying and practicing these skills. Understanding that these abilities can be developed empowers you to take control of your learning journey rather than feeling defeated by a perceived lack of natural talent.

Fundamental Principles of Nonverbal Communication

To effectively learn nonverbal communication, starting with the basics is essential. Several key theories and principles form the foundation of this field. For instance, the concept of proxemics, introduced by anthropologist Edward T. Hall, explores how physical space impacts interactions. Recognizing personal space boundaries can help you navigate social situations more comfortably.

Additionally, understanding kinesics, the study of body movements, gestures, and facial expressions, provides insight into what people might feel or think without uttering a word. Mastering these elements requires keen observation and practice but opens up a new dimension in understanding human behavior.

Another crucial principle is paralanguage, which includes tone, pitch, and speech volume. These vocal elements often convey more emotions and intentions than words spoken. By paying attention to paralanguage, you can gain deeper insights into someone's feelings.

A Scientific Approach to Learning

While intuition might play a minor role in interpreting nonverbal cues, relying solely on it can lead to misinterpretations. Instead, adopting a scientific approach ensures accuracy and reliability in your interpretations. Start by observing patterns in different contexts—notice how people behave in various social settings and try to deduce common themes.

Engaging with academic resources on psychology and behavioral science will also enhance your understanding. Numerous studies provide evidence-based strategies for interpreting nonverbal signals accurately. For example, Paul Ekman's work on facial expressions categorizes universal emotions recognizable across cultures.

Practical application is key to solidifying your skills further. Regularly practice observing interactions around you—at work, social gatherings, or even through media like movies or TV shows—and test your interpretations against actual outcomes or feedback from others.

Empowering Your Journey

It's important to remember that improving your ability to read nonverbal cues is a gradual process that requires patience and persistence. Every small improvement brings you closer to mastering this silent language. Embrace each learning opportunity as a step forward rather than focusing on setbacks or mistakes.

Taking control of your learning process with a structured approach rooted in science will enhance your communication skills and build stronger personal and professional relationships. The journey may seem challenging initially, but anyone can proficiently interpret nonverbal communication with dedication and practice.

In this chapter's exploration of nonverbal communication's scientific basis, you'll discover practical strategies for honing these skills effectively. Remember: these abilities are not exclusive talents but attainable skills waiting for you to unlock through guided learning and consistent practice.

Your journey towards mastering the secrets of human behavior through nonverbal cues begins here—armed with knowledge and determination, you're ready to decode the silent language that connects us all.

Nonverbal communication is often mistakenly perceived as an innate skill, a mysterious ability that some are born with while others are not. The truth, however, is that interpreting nonverbal cues is a learned skill rooted in psychology and behavioral science. This misconception can lead individuals to believe they cannot understand body language, facial expressions, and other nonverbal signals. The good news is that these abilities are not exclusive gifts but learnable skills that anyone can acquire with guidance and practice.

By debunking the myth of inherent intuition in nonverbal communication, we can shift the narrative towards a more empowering truth: the ability to read nonverbal cues is within reach for everyone. It's essential to recognize that, like any other skill, mastering nonverbal communication requires dedication and effort. Instead of feeling discouraged by the misconception of innate talent, individuals should embrace the idea that they can enhance their understanding of nonverbal cues through education and practice.

Understanding the science behind nonverbal communication can demystify this complex language and make it more accessible. By emphasizing the learnable nature of interpreting nonverbal cues, we encourage individuals to embark on a journey of discovery and growth in their social interactions. This shift in perspective opens up a world of possibilities for improving relationships, enhancing emotional intelligence, and navigating social dynamics confidently.

Fundamental Principles and Theories of Nonverbal Communication

Some fundamental principles and theories are the foundation for understanding human behavior in nonverbal communication. We can unravel the intricate web of unspoken cues that shape our interactions with others by delving into these basic concepts. One key principle is the universality of certain nonverbal expressions, such as facial expressions of happiness, sadness, anger, and fear. These expressions transcend cultural boundaries, making them essential cues for interpreting emotions accurately.

Another critical theory in nonverbal communication is body language, which encompasses gestures, posture, and movement. Our bodies often reveal more than words, providing valuable insights into our thoughts and feelings. Understanding how to decipher these bodily signals can significantly enhance our ability to connect with others on a deeper level.

Eye contact is yet another crucial aspect of nonverbal communication. The eyes are the windows to the soul, offering a glimpse into a person's intentions and emotions. Maintaining appropriate eye contact conveys confidence and attentiveness while avoiding eye contact can signal discomfort or dishonesty. By honing our ability to interpret eye movements and gaze patterns, we can glean valuable information about others' inner states.

Proxemics, or the study of personal space and distance between individuals, is also a key element in nonverbal communication. Different cultures have varying norms regarding personal space, with some valuing closer proximity during interactions than others. Being mindful of these cultural differences can prevent misunderstandings and promote respectful communication across diverse contexts.

Nonverbal cues play a significant role in regulating social interactions. They can convey interest, empathy, dominance, submission, or many other messages without uttering words. Becoming proficient in decoding these cues empowers us to navigate social situations more easily and effectively.

Micro expressions, fleeting facial expressions that reveal genuine emotions before individuals can mask them, are another essential component of nonverbal communication. These brief flashes of emotion can provide valuable clues about someone's true feelings, helping us to discern sincerity from deception.

In mastering the basic principles and theories governing nonverbal communication, we equip ourselves with invaluable tools for deciphering the silent language that permeates our daily interactions. Developing a keen awareness of these cues and practicing their interpretation regularly can enhance our emotional intelligence and forge stronger connections with those around us.

Scientific Approach to Interpreting Nonverbal Cues

In understanding nonverbal communication, a scientific approach is key to unraveling the intricacies of human behavior. By adopting a structured framework, individuals can effectively enhance their ability to interpret and respond to nonverbal cues. This descriptive framework is designed to assist in recognizing, decoding, and utilizing nonverbal signals within various social contexts.

Recognition Phase: Detecting Cues

The first step in the framework involves the recognition phase, where individuals observe and identify nonverbal cues displayed by others. This phase emphasizes the importance of attentive observation and heightened awareness of facial expressions, body language, gestures, and spatial positioning. **By honing these observational skills**, individuals can gather valuable information about the emotions, intentions, and attitudes of those they interact with.

Interpretation Phase: Understanding Meanings

Once cues are recognized, the interpretation phase comes into play. This stage requires individuals to analyze and interpret the potential meanings behind the observed nonverbal signals. By considering context, cultural nuances, and individual differences, individuals can gain deeper insights into the underlying messages conveyed through nonverbal communication.

Reaction Phase: Choosing Appropriate Responses

The final phase of the framework focuses on the reaction stage, where individuals select appropriate responses based on their interpretations of nonverbal cues. This phase involves responding empathetically to others' nonverbal signals, adapting communication styles, and establishing rapport through mirroring and synchrony. By choosing responses that align with the perceived emotional states of others, individuals can foster better connections and understanding in their interactions.

Dynamic Interplay of Components

The components of this framework interact dynamically, forming a cohesive system for navigating social interactions. The recognition phase feeds into the interpretation phase, guiding responses in the reaction phase. This cyclical process allows continuous feedback and adjustment based on ongoing observations and interpretations of nonverbal cues.

Practical Implications

Practical applications of this framework extend across various domains, including professional settings like leadership and negotiation, social interactions such as making new acquaintances, and intimate relationships where maintaining rapport is crucial. By applying this scientific approach to interpreting nonverbal cues, individuals can enhance their emotional intelligence, build stronger connections with others, and navigate social situations with confidence.

Individuals can better understand human behavior and improve interpersonal relationships by embracing a scientific approach to decoding nonverbal communication through this framework model. Through focused practice and applying these principles in real-world scenarios, readers can unlock the secrets of human interaction and elevate their communication skills to new heights.

Understanding nonverbal communication is not a talent reserved for a select few; it is a skill anyone can learn and refine. The myth that these abilities are purely intuitive undermines the potential for growth and mastery in this area. Recognizing that nonverbal cues are governed by principles and theories rooted in psychology and behavioral science opens the door to systematic learning and improvement.

Embracing a scientific approach allows you to break down the complex world of nonverbal communication into manageable, actionable steps. You have the foundational knowledge to build upon, transforming perceived intuition into reliable, evidence-based skills. Remember, it's about practice and perseverance, not innate ability.

The journey to mastering nonverbal cues starts with awareness and understanding. You can enhance your emotional intelligence and interpret the silent language of human behavior more effectively by applying what you've learned here. Take control of this learning process; you'll see tangible improvements with consistent effort.

As you delve into the subsequent chapters, remember that each piece of knowledge builds upon the last. The more you practice and observe, the clearer these nonverbal signals will become. Your dedication to mastering these skills will improve your interactions and empower you to navigate social situations confidently and quickly.

Stay curious, stay observant, and most importantly, keep practicing. The ability to decode nonverbal communication is within your reach—embrace the challenge and unlock your potential.

Chapter 4: Across the Cultural Divide: Navigating Nonverbal Nuances

"Good communication is just as stimulating

as black coffee and just as hard

to sleep after."

Anne Morrow Lindbergh

Discover the Hidden Meanings in Nonverbal Cues Across Cultures

Nonverbal communication is crucial to human interaction, often conveying more than words. However, these cues are not universally understood; they can vary significantly from one culture to another. Imagine a friendly gesture in your country being perceived as rude or offensive elsewhere. This chapter delves into the fascinating world of cultural variability in nonverbal communication, offering vital insights for anyone navigating our increasingly globalized society.

Understanding how nonverbal cues differ across cultures is not just an academic exercise; it has real-world implications for cross-cultural interactions. For instance, while a thumbs-up gesture might be seen as a positive affirmation in many Western cultures, it can be offensive in parts of the Middle East. Recognizing these differences helps prevent misunderstandings leading to conflicts or strained relationships.

In today's interconnected world, cultural sensitivity is more important than ever. Misinterpreting nonverbal signals can lead to awkward situations or even damage professional and personal relationships. Awareness of these differences can foster more effective communication and build stronger connections with people from diverse backgrounds.

This chapter will provide practical tools to avoid common pitfalls in cross-cultural communication. One key strategy is to observe and learn from locals in a new cultural setting. Pay close attention to their body language, facial expressions, and other nonverbal cues. This observational approach allows you to pick up on subtle nuances that may not be immediately apparent.

Another essential tactic is asking questions when unsure about a particular gesture or expression. People generally appreciate it when you show interest in their culture and try to understand it better. This helps clarify potential misunderstandings and demonstrates your respect and willingness to learn.

Adapting your own nonverbal behavior is also crucial for successful cross-cultural interactions. If you know that certain gestures or expressions are viewed differently in another culture, consciously adjust your behavior. This adaptability shows cultural competence and enhances your ability to communicate effectively with others.

Lastly, embracing continuous learning is vital for mastering cross-cultural nonverbal communication. Cultures are dynamic and constantly evolving, so staying updated on these changes is essential. Engage with cultural resources such as books, documentaries, or conversations with people from different backgrounds to keep your knowledge fresh and relevant.

By the end of this chapter, you'll have a deeper understanding of how nonverbal communication varies across cultures and practical strategies for navigating these differences. You'll be better equipped to interpret the silent language of human behavior accurately and build meaningful connections in our diverse world.

Nonverbal communication is vital to human interaction, but its nuances vary significantly across cultures. What may be considered a friendly gesture in one culture could be seen as disrespectful in another. Understanding these cultural differences is crucial for navigating cross-cultural interactions successfully. Body language, facial expressions, gestures, and even eye contact can all carry different meanings depending on the cultural context. For instance, while direct eye contact is often viewed as a sign of confidence and attentiveness in Western cultures, it can be interpreted as confrontational or disrespectful in some Asian cultures.

These variations in nonverbal communication can lead to misunderstandings and misinterpretations. Imagine a scenario where a person from a culture that values personal space stands close to someone from a culture that prefers more physical distance during conversations. Individuals with different cultural backgrounds might perceive closeness as intrusive or aggressive. At the same time, the other person may see the distance as cold or indifferent. Recognizing and respecting these differences can help avoid unnecessary conflicts and foster better understanding.

In addition to physical proximity, hand gestures, facial expressions, and even the tone of voice can convey different meanings across cultures. A thumbs-up gesture that signifies approval in one culture might be offensive in another. Similarly, smiling can have varying interpretations – from friendliness to nervousness or insincerity. Being aware of these variations is essential for effective communication. It's not just about what is said but also how it is expressed nonverbally that influences how a message is received.

Cross-cultural interactions require sensitivity and adaptability. It's essential to approach interactions with an open mind and willingness to learn about different cultural norms regarding nonverbal cues. Being observant and respectful of these differences can build stronger connections with individuals from diverse backgrounds. Remember that communication is not just about words; it's about understanding the unspoken messages contributing to effective dialogue.

Strategies for Cultivating Cultural Sensitivity in Nonverbal Communication

Cultural sensitivity is vital to effective communication, especially regarding nonverbal cues. Avoiding misconceptions in cross-cultural interactions requires a deep understanding of the nuances between different cultural norms. To foster cultural sensitivity, it is essential to approach interactions with an open mind and a willingness to learn from others' perspectives.

One practical insight for navigating cultural differences in nonverbal communication is to observe and adapt. Pay close attention to the nonverbal cues exhibited by individuals from different cultures. Be mindful of gestures, facial expressions, and body language with varying interpretations across cultures. By observing and adapting your own nonverbal behavior, you can show respect for diverse cultural practices and avoid unintentionally causing offense.

Empathy plays a crucial role in fostering cultural sensitivity. Put yourself in the shoes of someone from a different cultural background and try to understand their perspective. Recognize that what may seem natural or appropriate in one culture could be perceived differently in another. By approaching interactions with empathy and a genuine desire to connect, you can bridge the gap created by cultural differences and build meaningful relationships.

Another practical strategy for enhancing cultural sensitivity in nonverbal communication is to seek feedback. Don't hesitate to ask individuals from different cultures for feedback on your nonverbal cues. They can provide valuable insights into how your gestures, expressions, or tone may be perceived within their cultural context. By actively seeking feedback and being open to constructive criticism, you demonstrate a commitment to improving your cross-cultural communication skills.

Education is key to fostering cultural sensitivity in nonverbal communication. Take the time to learn about the cultural norms and practices of the individuals you interact with regularly. This could involve reading books, attending workshops, or conversing with people from diverse cultural backgrounds. By educating yourself on different cultural perspectives, you can navigate nonverbal nuances more effectively and show respect for varying ways of expression.

In summary, navigating nonverbal nuances across cultures requires a combination of observation, adaptation, empathy, feedback-seeking, and education. By incorporating these practical insights into your interactions, you can avoid misconceptions and foster greater cultural sensitivity. Remember that every interaction presents an opportunity to learn and grow your understanding of nonverbal communication within a multicultural world.

Navigating through different cultural norms regarding nonverbal cues can be challenging. Still, with the right strategies, it can become a smoother process. One essential approach is active observation. You can start picking up patterns and understanding their meanings by paying close attention. This observant attitude helps in learning through immersion.

Engaging with individuals from diverse cultural backgrounds allows you to practice adapting to various nonverbal communication styles. It's crucial to approach these interactions with an open mind and a willingness to learn. Asking questions respectfully about the meanings behind certain gestures or expressions can also be enlightening and show your interest in understanding their culture.

Another effective strategy is seeking feedback. After an interaction where nonverbal cues played a significant role, asking for feedback from someone familiar with that culture can provide valuable insights into any misunderstandings or misinterpretations that might have occurred. This feedback loop helps in fine-tuning your nonverbal communication skills for future interactions.

Moreover, educating yourself about different cultural practices and norms related to nonverbal communication is crucial. Resources like books, documentaries, or even online articles can provide valuable information on various cultural nuances. This proactive approach demonstrates your commitment to cultural sensitivity and fosters better cross-cultural communication.

When uncertain about a particular nonverbal cue or gesture, pausing and reflecting before reacting is beneficial. Considering the situation's context and the person's cultural background can prevent misunderstandings and promote cultural awareness. This reflective practice encourages empathy and shows respect for diverse ways of expressing emotions and intentions.

In addition, practicing mindfulness can enhance your ability to stay present during cross-cultural interactions and pick up on subtle nonverbal cues effectively. Being mindful of your own body language and facial expressions while also being attuned to those of others can significantly improve cross-cultural communication.

Lastly, embracing curiosity is key to navigating different cultural norms regarding nonverbal cues. Cultivating a genuine interest in learning about other cultures enriches your understanding. It strengthens your ability to connect authentically with individuals from diverse backgrounds. Curiosity opens the door to new experiences and fosters empathetic connections, bridging the gap across cultural divides in nonverbal communication.

Understanding nonverbal communication across cultures is more than an academic exercise; it is an essential skill for effective interaction in our increasingly interconnected world. Nonverbal cues are often the unspoken language that bridges—or divides—cultural gaps. By recognizing that these cues can vary significantly, you pave the way for clearer and more respectful communication.

Cultural sensitivity in nonverbal communication isn't just about avoiding misunderstandings; it's about fostering genuine connections. You demonstrate respect and empathy when acknowledging and adapting to cultural norms. This not only enhances personal relationships but also strengthens professional collaborations. Empathy and awareness are your best tools in navigating these complex interactions.

Equipped with practical strategies, you're better prepared to engage with diverse cultures more thoughtfully. Remember, *learning and adapting* to new nonverbal norms requires patience and openness. As you practice these strategies, you'll become more adept at reading the silent language of others, thus enhancing your overall emotional intelligence.

You have the innate ability to master these skills. With dedication, you can turn potential pitfalls into opportunities for deeper understanding and connection. Embrace this journey confidently, knowing that every step you take towards cultural competence enriches your growth and ability to connect meaningfully with others.

Applying what you've learned in this chapter, you'll avoid misconceptions and build a foundation of mutual respect and understanding. This approach will serve you well in all areas of life, from personal interactions to global business dealings. Take control of your learning journey—your commitment to understanding nonverbal nuances will lead to more effective and empathetic communication across cultures.

Chapter 5: Context is King: The Crucial Role of Situational Awareness

"Speak clearly, if you speak at all; carve every word

before you let it fall."

Oliver Wendell Holmes Sr.

Why Context Matters in Nonverbal Communication

Interpreting nonverbal cues without considering the context is like trying to understand a foreign language with only half the vocabulary. The gestures, facial expressions, and body language we rely on to communicate silently are deeply influenced by the situations in which they occur. Ignoring this context can lead to misunderstandings and misinterpretations, making it essential to factor in surrounding circumstances for accurate readings.

Nonverbal signals don't exist in a vacuum; they are part of a larger tapestry woven with threads of situational elements and cumulative behavior. For example, a smile during a heated debate carries a different meaning than one exchanged between friends at a casual gathering. Understanding this difference is crucial for interpreting the silent language effectively. Attention to the broader picture ensures that your interpretations align more closely with reality.

The Impact of Surrounding Circumstances

When focusing solely on isolated gestures or expressions, we risk missing the nuances that give those signals their true meaning. Surrounding circumstances provide the backdrop against which nonverbal cues make sense. A nod might signify agreement in one setting but could indicate mere acknowledgment in another. Therefore, it's about what is communicated and where and when it occurs.

To interpret nonverbal communication accurately, consider both immediate and extended contexts. Immediate context includes location, current activity, and who else is present. Extended context covers broader influences such as cultural norms, past interactions, and individual personality traits. This comprehensive approach lets you decode signals more precisely, leading to more authentic interactions.

Cumulative Behavior: The Key to Consistency

One-off gestures can be misleading if viewed in isolation. Instead, look at cumulative behavior—the pattern of actions over time—to get a clearer picture of someone's true feelings or intentions. Suppose someone frequently avoids eye contact during conversations. In that case, it might suggest discomfort or evasiveness rather than a momentary lapse of attention.

By observing these patterns, you can differentiate between genuine signals and anomalies. For instance, if an otherwise calm colleague suddenly exhibits nervous habits during a meeting, it could indicate stress or anxiety specific to that situation. This awareness helps you tailor your responses more effectively, fostering better communication and understanding.

Embracing a Holistic Approach

To master nonverbal communication, adopt a holistic approach that integrates multiple elements of context and cumulative behavior. This strategy ensures that your interpretations are grounded in reality rather than assumptions. Consider not just the immediate gestures but also the environment, past interactions, and overall behavioral patterns.

Viewing nonverbal cues through this comprehensive lens makes you more adept at reading between the lines and responding appropriately. This skill enhances personal and professional relationships by fostering genuine connections based on accurate understanding.

Practical Strategies for Contextual Interpretation

Here are some practical strategies to help you apply this holistic approach:

1. **Observe Patterns:** Keep track of recurring behaviors over time rather than focusing on isolated incidents.
2. **Consider Environment:** Take note of where the interaction occurs—public vs. private settings can influence behavior significantly.
3. **Factor in Relationships:** Understand the history and dynamics between individuals involved; past interactions often shape present behaviors.
4. **Cultural Sensitivity:** Be aware of cultural norms that may affect how certain nonverbal cues are expressed and interpreted.

By implementing these strategies, you'll improve your ability to decode nonverbal communication accurately.

Cumulative Behavior and Surrounding Circumstances in Nonverbal Communication

Understanding nonverbal cues goes beyond isolated gestures; it involves considering the cumulative behavior and surrounding circumstances to interpret them accurately. A raised eyebrow may convey skepticism but could indicate agreement when paired with a nod. This interplay between different signals highlights the importance of looking at the bigger picture when decoding body language.

Cumulative behavior refers to the collection of nonverbal cues exhibited over time. Observing how gestures, expressions, and postures evolve during a conversation or interaction can gain valuable insights into a person's feelings and intentions. For example, a person who starts a conversation with open body language but gradually crosses their arms might signal discomfort or defensiveness. Attention to these subtle changes is crucial to grasp the full meaning behind nonverbal communication.

Moreover, surrounding circumstances play a significant role in shaping nonverbal signals. The environment, cultural norms, and interpersonal dynamics influence how gestures are interpreted. A smile at a funeral may not signify happiness but rather an attempt to comfort others. Similarly, standing close to someone in certain cultures may indicate friendliness, while others could see it as intrusive. Being mindful of these contextual factors helps avoid misinterpretations and fosters better communication.

By considering cumulative behavior and surrounding circumstances, individuals can enhance their ability to read nonverbal cues accurately. This holistic approach ensures that gestures and expressions are interpreted in light of the broader context, leading to more meaningful interactions. Rather than focusing solely on individual movements or facial expressions, this comprehensive view enables a deeper understanding of underlying emotions and intentions.

When deciphering nonverbal communication, observing patterns rather than isolated actions is essential. Look for consistency or changes in body language throughout an interaction to uncover hidden meanings. Additionally, being aware of cultural differences and adjusting interpretations based on the context can prevent misunderstandings and promote effective communication.

Remember that nonverbal cues do not exist in a vacuum; they are influenced by various factors that shape their meaning. By acknowledging the role of cumulative behavior and surrounding circumstances, individuals can navigate social interactions with greater insight and sensitivity. Developing this awareness allows for more authentic connections and smoother communication exchanges across diverse settings and relationships.

Adopting a holistic approach to reading signals for more authentic interactions is essential in understanding nonverbal communication. We can better understand the underlying messages by considering the context in which gestures, expressions, and behaviors occur. This comprehensive view enables us to interpret nonverbal cues more effectively and confidently navigate social situations.

Rather than focusing solely on individual gestures or expressions, it is crucial to consider the individual's surroundings and cumulative behavior. Context provides valuable insight into the meaning behind nonverbal signals, helping us avoid misinterpretations and misunderstandings. By examining the broader context of a situation, we can uncover hidden layers of communication that enhance our overall understanding.

One key aspect of adopting a holistic approach to reading nonverbal signals is recognizing that people communicate through verbal and nonverbal cues. Understanding how these different forms of communication interact can significantly impact our ability to decipher meaning accurately. We can better understand what is being communicated by paying attention to verbal and nonverbal signals within a conversation or interaction.

Additionally, a holistic approach involves being mindful of the environment in which communication occurs. Environmental factors such as noise levels, proximity between individuals, and cultural norms can all influence how nonverbal signals are perceived. Being aware of these contextual elements allows us to interpret nonverbal cues more accurately and accurately.

It is important to practice active listening and observation to encourage authentic interactions based on a holistic understanding of nonverbal communication. Engaging fully with verbal and nonverbal cues during interactions helps build rapport and fosters genuine connections. We can create more meaningful and fulfilling relationships by approaching communication with attentiveness and openness to contextual cues.

Adopting a holistic approach to reading nonverbal signals is essential for enhancing our interpersonal communication skills. By considering the context, cumulative behavior, environmental factors, and the interaction between verbal and nonverbal cues, we can decode messages more accurately and engage in authentic interactions. Practicing active listening and observation further strengthens our ability to connect with others on a deeper level, fostering empathy, understanding, and mutual respect in our social interactions.

Understanding the nuances of nonverbal communication requires an appreciation for the context in which these signals occur. The subtleties of body language, facial expressions, and gestures cannot be accurately interpreted without considering the surrounding circumstances and cumulative behavior. By emphasizing context, you can achieve a more authentic and effective interaction.

Cumulative behavior and situational awareness play pivotal roles in decoding nonverbal cues. A single gesture or expression might be misleading if taken out of context. However, when viewed as part of a broader pattern, these signals reveal more about underlying emotions and intentions. Recognizing these patterns allows you to respond more appropriately and build stronger connections.

Adopting a holistic approach to reading nonverbal signals ensures that your interpretations are grounded in reality. This involves paying attention to isolated gestures and the entire communicative environment. You can gain deeper insights into their true feelings by considering the speaker's history, emotional state, and specific situation.

Practical application of these principles can transform your interactions. Start by observing and noting patterns in behavior over time rather than jumping to conclusions based on a single action. Practice situational awareness by being mindful of your conversations' settings and circumstances. This will help you avoid misinterpretations and enhance your emotional intelligence.

Empower yourself with these strategies to take control of your interactions. Mastering contextual awareness allows you to navigate social situations more confidently and empathetically. Remember, understanding human behavior is not about deciphering isolated signals but about seeing the bigger picture that these signals paint together.

Incorporate these insights into your daily life to experience tangible improvements in your communication skills. Your ability to read between the lines will become sharper, leading to more meaningful and genuine connections with others.

Chapter 6: The Mehrabian Blueprint: Understanding Communication Composition

"The single biggest problem in communication is

the illusion that it has taken place."

George Bernard Shaw

Unlocking the Power of Nonverbal Communication

Albert Mehrabian's **7-38-55 Rule** is a revelation in understanding how we communicate. It suggests that only 7% of communication relies on our words. A striking 38% depends on our vocal elements and an overwhelming 55% hinges on body language. This chapter dives deep into Mehrabian's groundbreaking findings, emphasizing nonverbal cues' critical role in effective communication.

Understanding Mehrabian's Rule provides a framework for interpreting the silent language accompanying our spoken words. In everyday interactions, we often focus on what is being said without paying much attention to how it is said or what is being conveyed through gestures, facial expressions, and posture. Mehrabian's research underscores that these nonverbal elements are supplementary and often more telling than verbal messages.

Consider how often you've felt something was off in a conversation despite hearing agreeable words. This dissonance is usually due to conflicting nonverbal signals. When words say one thing but body language and tone convey another, it's the nonverbal message that people tend to trust more. This insight is not just academic; it has practical applications in daily life and professional settings.

Applying Mehrabian's Rule can transform your communication skills by making you more attuned to the silent language of others and more aware of the messages you send nonverbally. For instance, maintaining eye contact, adopting an open posture, and using appropriate facial expressions can significantly enhance your ability to connect with others. These subtle cues can convey empathy, confidence, and sincerity far more effectively than words alone.

In professional environments, understanding and utilizing nonverbal communication can be a game-changer. Whether leading a team meeting or negotiating a deal, your body language can reinforce or undermine your verbal messages if there's inconsistency. By aligning your verbal and nonverbal communication, you build trust and credibility—essential for successful interactions.

Moreover, this chapter will guide you through practical strategies to improve your nonverbal communication skills. You'll learn techniques for accurately reading others' body language and adjusting your own to communicate more effectively. These actionable insights will empower you to navigate social interactions more easily and confidently.

Mastering Mehrabian's Rule isn't about becoming hyper-vigilant or overly analytical of every gesture or tone but enhancing your awareness. Being mindful of the silent language accompanying spoken words enriches your understanding of human behavior and improves emotional intelligence. This holistic approach to communication ensures you're not just hearing but truly understanding those around you.

In summary, Mehrabian's 7-38-55 Rule offers invaluable insights into the composition of effective communication. You can become a more adept communicator by recognizing the dominant role of nonverbal cues and integrating this understanding into daily practice. This chapter equips you with the knowledge and tools needed to unlock these secrets of human behavior, paving the way for more meaningful connections and successful interactions in all areas of life.

Albert Mehrabian's 7-38-55 Rule sheds light on the intricate dynamics of human communication. According to this rule, only 7% of communication relies on spoken words. In comparison, 38% is attributed to vocal elements such as tone, pitch, and intonation. The staggering majority, 55%, pertains to body language – gestures, facial expressions, and posture. This rule underscores the importance of nonverbal cues in understanding and interpreting messages accurately in our daily interactions.

In our everyday exchanges, it is crucial to recognize that spoken words carry only a fraction of the message. The tone of voice and body language are pivotal in shaping the true intent behind the words uttered. Understanding Mehrabian's 7-38-55 Rule allows us to understand the significance of observing what is said and how it is expressed nonverbally.

Nonverbal cues often convey more profound meanings than verbal ones. Imagine a situation where someone says they are fine, but their crossed arms and furrowed brows suggest otherwise. In such instances, Mehrabian's rule becomes especially relevant as it highlights the need to pay attention to these subtle yet powerful indicators that reveal the underlying emotions and sentiments behind the spoken words.

By acknowledging and integrating Mehrabian's findings into our communication practices, we can better decipher others' unspoken messages. This enhanced awareness enables us to respond more effectively to what is communicated beyond mere words. As we delve deeper into Mehrabian's 7-38-55 Rule, we uncover insights that can significantly enrich our interpersonal connections and foster better understanding in our relationships.

The Impact of Mehrabian's 7-38-55 Rule on Effective Communication

Mehrabian's 7-38-55 Rule sheds light on the significant impact of nonverbal cues in communication. Understanding the dominance of body language in conveying messages is crucial for effective interactions. The rule highlights that words contribute only 7% of communication. In comparison, vocal elements make up 38%, and a staggering 55% is attributed to body language. This underscores the vital role that nonverbal cues play in how our messages are perceived by others.

Nonverbal cues such as facial expressions, gestures, posture, and eye contact often convey our feelings and intentions more than words alone. While verbal communication provides essential information, the nonverbal elements often carry the emotional weight of a message. Awareness of these nonverbal signals can significantly enhance our ability to understand others and express ourselves more effectively.

Facial expressions are particularly powerful indicators of emotions. A smile can communicate warmth and friendliness, while a furrowed brow may signal concern or displeasure. Understanding these subtle cues can help us interpret others' emotions accurately and respond appropriately. Additionally, body language, such as open gestures versus crossed arms or leaning in versus leaning away, can convey interest, attentiveness, defensiveness, or disengagement.

Mastering nonverbal communication involves decoding others' signals and being mindful of our body language. Projecting confidence through posture, making eye contact to show attentiveness, and mirroring the body language of others to build rapport are essential skills in effective communication. By honing our ability to read and use nonverbal cues, we can navigate social interactions with greater sensitivity and insight.

Developing proficiency in interpreting nonverbal cues can lead to more authentic connections with others. When we pay attention to what is said and how it is expressed nonverbally, we gain a more comprehensive understanding of the message being communicated. This heightened awareness allows for more nuanced and empathetic responses, fostering deeper relationships built on mutual understanding and trust.

Incorporating Mehrabian's insights into daily interactions can be transformative. Recognizing the significance of nonverbal cues allows us to fine-tune our communication skills, leading to clearer exchanges and stronger connections with those around us. Through practice and observation, we can become adept at deciphering the silent language of body movements and facial expressions, enhancing our emotional intelligence and enriching our relationships.

Now that we have delved into the nuances of Mehrabian's 7-38-55 Rule and the significance of nonverbal cues in communication, it is time to equip you with actionable strategies to enhance your communication skills effectively.

- **Practice Active Listening:** Active listening is one of the most crucial elements of effective communication. By focusing on the speaker, maintaining eye contact, and displaying open body language, you show genuine interest in what the other person is saying. This not only fosters better understanding but also strengthens rapport and connection.

- **Observe Nonverbal Cues:** Pay attention to nonverbal cues in your interactions. Notice gestures, facial expressions, and posture to better understand what others are communicating beyond words. This heightened awareness can help you respond appropriately and empathetically.

- **Mirror Positivity:** Use positive body language to convey openness and receptiveness. Smile genuinely, nod in agreement, and maintain an upright posture to signal confidence and attentiveness. Mirroring positive cues can create a harmonious atmosphere and encourage smoother communication exchanges.

- **Seek Feedback:** Actively seek feedback on your nonverbal communication from trusted individuals. They can provide valuable insights into how your body language is perceived and offer constructive suggestions for improvement. Embracing feedback is a powerful tool for enhancing self-awareness and refining your communication style.

- **Practice Empathy:** Cultivate empathy by putting yourself in the other person's shoes. Consider their perspective, emotions, and unspoken cues to respond with compassion and understanding. Empathy builds trust and strengthens connections by showing that you value the other person's feelings.

- **Use Visual Aids:** When presenting information or ideas, incorporate visual aids such as charts, graphs, or images to complement your verbal message. Visual cues can enhance comprehension, retention, and engagement, making your communication more impactful and memorable.

- **Role-Play Scenarios:** Engage in role-playing exercises to practice interpreting and conveying nonverbal cues effectively. Simulating real-life scenarios with a partner or group can refine your observation skills, adaptability, and responsiveness in various communication contexts.

By implementing these practical strategies into your daily interactions, you can harness the power of Mehrabian's 7-38-55 Rule to enhance your communication skills significantly. Remember that mastering nonverbal communication is an ongoing process that requires dedication and mindfulness. With consistent practice and application, you will become adept at decoding body language, fostering deeper connections, and navigating social interactions confidently and authentically.

As we wrap up our exploration of Mehrabian's 7-38-55 Rule, we must recognize the profound impact nonverbal communication has on our daily interactions. Mehrabian's findings underscore that a mere 7% of communication is conveyed through words. In comparison, vocal elements account for 38%, and a staggering 55% is expressed through body language. This insight alone should reshape how we approach our conversations and relationships.

Nonverbal cues are not just supplementary; they are essential. They form the foundation upon which effective communication is built. From subtle gestures to facial expressions and posture, these silent signals often convey more than spoken words ever could. Understanding and mastering these cues can transform your ability to connect with others, making your interactions more meaningful and impactful.

By applying Mehrabian's rule, you can begin to truly listen with your eyes and ears. Pay attention to the nuances of tone and voice inflection, but more importantly, observe the accompanying body language. Are the person's words aligned with their gestures? Is there congruence between what they say and how they are saying it? These observations will enable you to discern underlying emotions and intentions that might go unnoticed.

A practical application starts with mindfulness. Begin by observing your own nonverbal behaviors. Are you sending mixed signals? Practice aligning your body language with verbal messages to ensure clarity and authenticity. As you become more attuned to these aspects within yourself, extend this awareness to others.

Encourage yourself to engage actively with these strategies. Start small—perhaps by focusing on maintaining open body language during conversations or consciously modulating your tone of voice to match the emotional context of your message. Over time, these practices will become second nature, enriching personal and professional relationships.

Remember, you have the inherent ability to master this skill set. Nonverbal communication is not a mystery; it's a learnable art form. You can significantly enhance your emotional intelligence and interpersonal effectiveness with deliberate practice and a keen awareness of Mehrabian's insights.

In summary, embracing the principles outlined in this chapter will empower you to communicate more effectively by harnessing the power of nonverbal cues. Take control of this aspect of communication—your relationships will benefit immensely from this newfound clarity and depth in interaction.

Chapter 7: The Flicker of Truth: Mastering Micro-expressions

"Communication leads to community, that is,

to understanding, intimacy, and

mutual valuing."

Rollo May

Discovering the Hidden Truths in Every Face

A significant part of human interaction is communicated without words. Micro-expressions—fleeting, involuntary facial movements that pass in the blink of an eye—are crucial to this silent dialogue. According to Paul Ekman's pioneering work, these brief flashes of genuine emotion can reveal truths that words often conceal. Recognizing and interpreting micro-expressions can unlock a deeper understanding of those around us, offering insights into their true feelings and intentions.

Understanding micro-expressions starts with recognizing their significance. Unlike broader body language cues or more prolonged facial expressions, micro-expressions occur in less than half a second and are almost impossible to fake. They are the raw, unfiltered emotional responses that seep through despite our best efforts to mask them. This makes them incredibly valuable for anyone looking to understand another's emotional state, whether in personal relationships, professional environments, or even during negotiations.

Paul Ekman's research has shown that these expressions are universal, transcending cultural and linguistic barriers. Whether you're interacting with someone from your hometown or halfway across the globe, a micro-expression of sadness or joy looks the same. This universality means that once you master the skill of recognizing these subtle cues, you can apply it universally. Imagine sensing a colleague's hidden frustration despite their polite words or detecting a friend's concealed delight regardless of their stoic demeanor.

To harness micro-expressions' power effectively, one must first learn to identify them accurately. This involves training oneself to notice these rapid changes in facial muscles that signal different emotions. Start by familiarizing yourself with Ekman's categorization of seven basic emotions: happiness, sadness, fear, disgust, anger, surprise, and contempt. Each has distinct micro-expressive markers—for instance, a fleeting frown signaling anger or a quick widening of the eyes indicating surprise.

Practical Steps for Real-Time Recognition

Developing the ability to recognize micro-expressions requires practice and patience. Begin by observing people during conversations—in person or through video recordings—and pay close attention to their faces when they react emotionally. Slow-motion playback can be particularly useful initially until you train your eyes to catch these rapid movements in real time.

Once you're comfortable identifying these micro-expressions, the next step is interpreting them within context. A single micro-expression alone may not provide the full story. Combined with other nonverbal cues like body language and tone of voice, it becomes part of a larger narrative about someone's emotional state. For example, suppose someone expresses a brief flash of fear followed by tightening their lips and avoiding eye contact. In that case, it might indicate anxiety or discomfort about the topic.

Applying Your Skills

Using these skills effectively involves more than just detection; it also requires a tactful response. Consider how you might address the underlying emotion constructively when you notice a micro-expression. If you see signs of stress in a colleague during a meeting—such as fleeting expressions of fear or sadness—you might offer support or ask if they need help.

Remember that while micro-expressions are powerful tools for understanding others better, they should be used ethically and compassionately. The goal is not to manipulate but to foster deeper connections and more authentic interactions by being attuned to others' true feelings.

Mastering micro-expressions can transform how you perceive and interact with others personally and professionally. By honing this skill, you empower yourself with an enhanced ability to navigate complex social landscapes with greater empathy and insight. As you continue interpreting silent language, you'll find that every face tells a story waiting to be understood—often far more accurately than words ever could convey.

Micro-expressions are the fleeting, involuntary facial expressions that give us a glimpse into someone's true emotions. They occur in a fraction of a second, often revealing what a person feels beneath their spoken words. Understanding and interpreting these micro-expressions can be a powerful tool in deciphering genuine emotions and intentions in various interactions. While we may consciously control our facial expressions to some extent, micro-expressions bypass our conscious efforts, making them a more reliable indicator of true feelings.

The Significance of Micro-Expressions

In social interactions, where words can be deceiving or ambiguous, micro-expressions act as unfiltered truth-tellers. Imagine detecting subtle signs of discomfort, joy, or deceit in real-time, giving you an edge in understanding the people around you more deeply. Recognizing micro-expressions allows us to connect more authentically by responding to what is said and the genuine emotions behind the words.

Micro-expressions are like hidden messages waiting to be decoded. By mastering the skill of reading these rapid facial movements, we equip ourselves with invaluable insights that go beyond surface interactions. It's akin to having a secret decoder for human emotions, enabling us to navigate social situations with heightened awareness and sensitivity.

Unlocking Genuine Emotions

Deciphering micro-expressions can lead to profound connections and improved communication skills. By honing this skill, we enhance our emotional intelligence and sharpen our understanding of others' feelings. Stay tuned as we delve deeper into the universal nature of micro-expressions according to Paul Ekman's groundbreaking theory and explore practical methods for recognizing and interpreting these subtle yet revealing cues in real-time interactions.

As Paul Ekman proposed, micro-expressions are fleeting facial expressions that reveal genuine emotions. One of the key aspects of micro-expressions is their universal nature. According to Ekman's theory, these brief expressions are consistent across cultures and individuals, providing a window into someone's true feelings. This universality underscores the importance of understanding and interpreting micro-expressions in our interactions.

Ekman's research has shown that micro-expressions transcend language barriers and cultural differences. Whether you are in New York or Tokyo, a smile of genuine happiness or a flash of anger will be displayed similarly on a person's face. This universality allows us to tap into a shared language of emotions, enabling us to connect more deeply with those around us.

Recognizing micro-expression universality can empower us to navigate social interactions with greater insight and empathy. By honing our ability to identify these fleeting signals, we can better understand people's true emotions and intentions. This awareness can help us build more authentic connections and foster trust in our relationships.

Deciphering micro-expressions can be especially beneficial in professional settings, where clear communication and understanding are paramount. By recognizing subtle cues in facial expressions, we can better grasp the underlying emotions driving our colleagues' behavior. This insight can enhance teamwork, improve conflict resolution, and create a more harmonious work environment.

Understanding the universal nature of micro-expressions also equips us with a valuable tool for emotional intelligence. By being attuned to these subtle cues, we can develop a heightened sense of empathy and insight into the emotions of those around us. This increased emotional intelligence can lead to more effective communication, conflict resolution, and stronger interpersonal relationships.

Incorporating the knowledge of universal micro-expressions into our daily interactions allows us to communicate more effectively and empathetically. We can deepen our connections with others and create more meaningful relationships by paying attention to these fleeting signals. Recognizing micro-expression universality is about decoding facial cues and fostering genuine understanding and connection with those we interact with daily.

In essence, mastering the understanding of universal micro-expressions provides a powerful tool for enhancing our emotional intelligence and navigating social interactions with greater sensitivity and insight. Through this awareness, we can connect with others on a deeper level, fostering authentic relationships built on mutual understanding and empathy.

Recognizing and interpreting micro-expressions in real-time interactions can be a game-changer in understanding the true emotions behind people's words. These fleeting facial expressions, often lasting only a fraction of a second, provide invaluable insights into someone's genuine feelings. To master the art of decoding micro-expressions, paying close attention to subtle cues and practicing your observation skills diligently is essential.

One method for recognizing micro-expressions is to focus on the eyes and mouth. These areas of the face are particularly expressive and can reveal much about a person's emotional state. Watch for quick movements, twitches, or changes in these regions, as they can indicate underlying emotions the individual may try to conceal.

- **Another effective technique** is to observe clusters of micro-expressions rather than isolated ones. By paying attention to patterns of facial movements and expressions over time, you can gain a more comprehensive understanding of someone's emotional landscape. Look for consistency or discrepancies in these micro-expressions to uncover hidden truths.

- **Practice active listening** while observing micro-expressions. Paying attention to what someone says and how they say it can provide valuable context for interpreting their emotions accurately. Combining verbal cues with nonverbal micro-expressions can paint a more complete picture of the person's inner world.

- **Engage in role-playing exercises** to sharpen your skills in recognizing and interpreting micro-expressions. By simulating real-life scenarios and practicing observation techniques in a controlled environment, you can improve your ability to pick up on subtle emotional cues and respond effectively in various social situations.

- **Seek feedback** from trusted friends or mentors on your progress in reading micro-expressions. Constructive criticism and external perspectives can help refine your observational skills and improve your accuracy in deciphering hidden emotions. Embrace opportunities for growth and learning from others' insights.

- **Maintain a curious mindset** when observing micro-expressions. Approach each interaction with an open attitude and a willingness to learn from every encounter. Cultivating curiosity about human behavior and emotions can deepen your understanding of nonverbal communication cues and enhance emotional intelligence.

By implementing these practical methods for recognizing and interpreting micro-expressions, you can hone your ability to read people more effectively and gain deeper insights into their true feelings. Remember that mastering this skill takes time and practice. Be patient with yourself as you embark on this journey toward greater emotional intelligence.

Understanding micro-expressions offers an invaluable key to unlocking the hidden layers of human emotion. These fleeting, involuntary facial expressions provide a direct window into someone's true feelings, often revealing what words cannot. By mastering the ability to recognize and interpret these subtle cues, you can significantly enhance your emotional intelligence and interpersonal skills.

Paul Ekman's pioneering research underscores the universal nature of micro-expressions, transcending cultural and linguistic barriers. This universality means you can apply this knowledge in any context or interaction once you grasp these expressions. In personal relationships or professional settings, recognizing micro-expressions equips you with a deeper awareness of others' emotions, fostering more genuine and empathetic connections.

But awareness alone isn't enough; practical application is key. You can improve your accuracy in real-time interactions by actively practicing the techniques discussed—such as paying close attention to brief facial movements and correlating them with underlying emotions. Catching these micro-moments allows you to respond more thoughtfully and effectively, whether navigating a complex negotiation or deepening a personal relationship.

Remember, the journey toward mastering micro-expressions is gradual. Start by observing those around you in everyday situations. Practice consistently, and soon, you'll find yourself more attuned to the silent signals people send. This skill doesn't just make you a better observer; it transforms how you interact with the world, making your communication more authentic and impactful.

By integrating these insights into your daily life, you'll become adept at reading others and more mindful of your nonverbal cues. This dual awareness fosters a richer understanding of human behavior and enhances your ability to connect more deeply. Embrace this journey with patience and curiosity, knowing that each step brings you closer to mastering the silent language of micro-expressions.

Chapter 8: The Five Pillars of Emotional Intelligence: Building Your EI Blueprint

"The way we communicate with others and

with ourselves ultimately determines

the quality of our lives."

Tony Robbins

Elevate Your Emotional Intelligence: A Blueprint for Success

In a world where communication often transcends words, understanding the silent language of human behavior is paramount. Emotional intelligence (EI) is the cornerstone of this understanding, offering a framework to decode and respond effectively to others' emotions. Daniel Goleman, a renowned psychologist, outlines five key components of emotional intelligence: self-awareness, self-regulation, motivation, empathy, and social skills. Mastering these elements can significantly enhance one's ability to interpret nonverbal cues and engage in meaningful interactions.

Self-awareness serves as the foundation of emotional intelligence. It involves recognizing and understanding your own emotions as they occur. By becoming more attuned to your feelings, you can better manage your responses and interactions with others. Practical steps to develop self-awareness include regular self-reflection, maintaining a journal to track your emotional responses, and seeking feedback from trusted individuals. This practice allows you to identify patterns in your behavior and adjust them proactively.

Self-regulation is the ability to control or redirect disruptive emotions and impulses. It's about staying composed and thinking before acting. Techniques such as mindfulness meditation, deep-breathing exercises, and developing a pause-before-reacting habit can significantly enhance your self-regulation skills. When you can manage your emotional reactions effectively, it benefits you. It fosters a more positive environment for those around you.

The third component, motivation, goes beyond mere enthusiasm; it's about having an intrinsic drive to achieve goals for personal reasons rather than external rewards. Cultivating motivation involves setting clear, attainable goals and finding personal meaning in your tasks. Regularly revisiting your objectives and celebrating small victories can keep your motivation high despite challenges.

Empathy is perhaps the most crucial element for mastering nonverbal communication. It entails understanding others' emotions by putting yourself in their shoes. To enhance empathy, practice active listening without interrupting or judging. Pay close attention to body language and facial expressions during conversations. Engaging in perspective-taking exercises can also help you see situations from different viewpoints, fostering deeper connections with others.

Lastly, social skills encompass various abilities that facilitate effective interaction with others. This includes communication skills, conflict resolution capabilities, and building rapport. Improving social skills often involves practicing assertiveness without aggression, honing your ability to give and receive constructive feedback, and working on collaboration techniques within group settings.

Practical Steps Towards Mastery

By focusing on these five pillars of emotional intelligence—self-awareness, self-regulation, motivation, empathy, and social skills—you lay down a robust blueprint for enhancing verbal and nonverbal communication skills. The journey requires consistent effort but promises substantial rewards in personal growth and interpersonal relationships.

As you integrate these components into your daily life, you'll notice an improvement in how you understand others and how effectively you convey your feelings without words. Mastering these elements will make your interactions more meaningful and impactful, whether through a reassuring touch or an empathetic nod during a conversation.

Remember that developing emotional intelligence is an ongoing process. It's not about achieving perfection but about making continual progress toward becoming more emotionally attuned and responsive. By taking control of your emotional landscape through the practical strategies outlined here, you empower yourself to navigate the complexities of human behavior with greater ease and confidence.

Embrace this journey with patience and persistence. The silent language of human behavior holds immense power when interpreted correctly—and emotional intelligence is your key to unlocking that power effectively.

Emotional intelligence is a crucial skill that can significantly impact our personal and professional relationships. Daniel Goleman's framework outlines five key components of emotional intelligence: self-awareness, self-regulation, motivation, empathy, and social skills. These components serve as pillars that support our ability to understand and navigate the complex world of emotions in ourselves and others.

Self-awareness is the foundation of emotional intelligence. It involves recognizing and understanding our emotions, strengths, weaknesses, and triggers. Without self-awareness, managing our responses effectively in various situations becomes challenging. Self-regulation, the next component, builds on self-awareness by controlling impulsive reactions and managing emotions constructively. It enables us to think before we act and maintain composure even in stressful circumstances.

Motivation plays a vital role in driving us towards our goals and aspirations. In emotional intelligence, motivation refers to our drive to achieve beyond external rewards; it encompasses passion, resilience, and the ability to bounce back from setbacks. Empathy, often regarded as a cornerstone of emotional intelligence, involves understanding and sharing the feelings of others. Acknowledging their emotions and perspectives allows us to connect more deeply with people.

Finally, social skills round out the five components by focusing on how we interact with others. Strong social skills enable effective communication, conflict resolution, collaboration, and building meaningful relationships. These skills are essential for navigating social dynamics successfully in various contexts.

Enhancing Emotional Intelligence: Practical Tips for Each Pillar

Emotional intelligence is a skill that can be developed and honed over time with the right strategies and mindset. Each component of emotional intelligence plays a crucial role in our interactions with others and ourselves. Here are practical tips to help you enhance each of the five pillars of emotional intelligence:

Self-Awareness

Self-awareness is the foundation of emotional intelligence. To develop this pillar, start by regularly checking in with yourself. Take moments throughout the day to pause and reflect on your emotions, thoughts, and behaviors. Journaling can be a helpful tool in this process. Pay attention to your reactions and identify patterns in your responses. Becoming aware of your triggers and emotional cues will enable you to better understand yourself and how you relate to others.

Self-Regulation

Self-regulation involves managing your emotions effectively. Practice mindfulness techniques such as deep breathing, meditation, or progressive muscle relaxation to stay calm in stressful situations. When faced with a challenging emotion, step back before responding impulsively. Give yourself time to process your feelings and choose a constructive way to express them. Remember that you control how you react, even when emotions run high.

Motivation

Motivation is what drives us to achieve our goals. Cultivate a growth mindset by setting clear objectives and taking steps towards them daily. Find intrinsic sources of motivation by connecting your goals to your values and passions. Celebrate small victories along the way to maintain momentum. Surround yourself with supportive individuals encouraging and inspiring you to keep moving forward.

Empathy

Empathy is the ability to understand and share the feelings of others. Practice active listening by focusing on the speaker without interrupting or formulating your response while they speak. Put yourself in their shoes to see things from their perspective. Validate their emotions by acknowledging their feelings without judgment. Show empathy through gestures such as offering support, encouragement, or simply being present for them.

Social Skills

Social skills are essential for building strong relationships. Improve your communication skills by practicing assertiveness, active listening, and conflict-resolution techniques. Be attentive to nonverbal cues such as body language and facial expressions during conversations. Cultivate a positive attitude and approach interactions with openness and respect for others' viewpoints.

By dedicating time and effort to developing each component of emotional intelligence, you can enhance your ability to navigate social interactions effectively. Remember that progress takes time, so be patient with yourself as you work towards mastering these pillars of emotional intelligence. Embrace each opportunity for growth and learning as you strive to build a solid foundation for improved nonverbal communication skills in personal and professional settings.

EI Blueprint Framework: Enhancing Nonverbal Communication Skills

In understanding the Evaluation Framework for enhancing emotional intelligence in nonverbal communication, it is crucial to delve into each component's role and how they interact within the model. This framework aims to guide individuals toward self-improvement by breaking down emotional intelligence into manageable components. Let's explore each element in detail:

Self-Awareness:

Self-awareness is the foundation of emotional intelligence, allowing individuals to recognize their emotions and understand how they impact others. In nonverbal communication, self-awareness involves recognizing subtle cues in body language, facial expressions, and tone of voice. By honing this skill, individuals can better understand their emotional responses and adjust them accordingly when interacting with others.

Self-Regulation:

Self-regulation builds upon self-awareness by enabling individuals to manage their emotions effectively. Self-regulation empowers individuals to control their reactions to nonverbal cues in nonverbal communication, maintaining composure and responding thoughtfully. This component helps navigate social interactions smoothly and fosters positive connections based on emotional understanding rather than impulsive reactions.

Motivation:

Motivation plays a pivotal role in enhancing emotional intelligence for nonverbal communication. It involves fostering a positive attitude towards improving one's ability to interpret and respond to nonverbal cues effectively. Motivated individuals are driven to learn and grow in their understanding of emotions conveyed through nonverbal signals, ultimately leading to more meaningful interactions with others.

Empathy:

Empathy is a cornerstone of emotional intelligence, especially in nonverbal communication. It involves the ability to understand and share the feelings of others authentically. By cultivating empathy, individuals can develop a genuine sensitivity to the emotions conveyed through body language and facial expressions, fostering deeper connections and trust in interpersonal relationships.

Social Skills:

Social skills encompass the application of emotional insights to navigate social interactions successfully. In nonverbal communication, strong social skills enable individuals to adapt their communication style based on the emotional cues they perceive from others. This component facilitates effective collaboration, conflict resolution, and relationship-building through enhanced emotional intelligence.

Individuals can systematically assess and develop emotional intelligence by integrating these components within the Evaluation Framework to enhance nonverbal communication skills. Each element plays a vital role in shaping one's ability to interpret and respond to nonverbal cues effectively, ultimately leading to improved interpersonal connections and heightened emotional awareness.

Embrace this framework as a guide towards mastering emotional intelligence in nonverbal communication, empowering you to navigate social interactions confidently and authentically. Through self-awareness, self-regulation, motivation, empathy, and social skills, you can unlock the secrets of human behavior and cultivate meaningful relationships based on genuine emotional understanding.

Chapter 9: Seeing the Unseen: Sharpening Your Observation Skills

"Communication – the human connection – is the key

to personal and career success."

Paul J. Meyer

Unlock the Secrets of Human Behavior: Mastering Observation Skills

Developing keen observation skills is essential for interpreting nonverbal communication effectively. In a world where much of what we communicate is conveyed silently, the ability to read these cues can offer invaluable insights into people's true feelings and intentions. By honing your observation skills, you can become adept at picking up on subtle changes in behavior that might otherwise go unnoticed. This chapter will guide you through enhancing these skills, providing practical exercises, and emphasizing the importance of practice in various settings.

Observation skills are fundamental to understanding the silent language of human behavior. When we talk about nonverbal cues, we're referring to body language, facial expressions, gestures, posture, and even micro-expressions—brief, involuntary facial expressions that reveal genuine emotions. These cues are often more reliable than words because they are harder to control and fake. By becoming more observant, you'll be better equipped to interpret these signals accurately.

To sharpen your observation skills, start with simple exercises focusing on specific aspects of people's behavior. For example, spend a few minutes each day watching people in public places like parks or cafes. Take note of their posture, how they use their hands when they talk, and any repetitive movements they make. Initially, you might find it challenging to notice these details. Still, with consistent practice, your ability to observe will improve significantly.

Another effective exercise is to watch movies or TV shows with the sound off. This forces you to rely solely on visual cues to understand what is happening in a scene. Pay attention to the characters' body language and facial expressions—how they interact with one another without words. This practice will help you become more attuned to nonverbal communication and improve your interpretive skills.

Practicing observation in various settings is crucial for honing these skills further. Different environments offer different types of interactions and behaviors to observe. For instance, a corporate setting will present different nonverbal cues than a social gathering or a family event. By observing people across diverse contexts, you'll gain a broader understanding of how nonverbal communication varies depending on the situation.

It's also important to reflect on your observations regularly. Keep a journal where you jot down notes about what you've observed daily. This will help reinforce your learning and make it easier to spot patterns over time. Discussing your observations with others can provide new perspectives and enhance your understanding.

Lastly, remember that improving observation skills is an ongoing process. Consistency is key; the more you practice observing people and noting their behaviors, the more skilled you will become at interpreting nonverbal signals accurately. Don't be discouraged if progress seems slow at first—like any other skill, mastery comes with time and dedication.

Following these strategies and committing to regular practice, you'll develop keen observation skills essential for unlocking human behavior's secrets. Not only will this enhance your ability to read nonverbal cues accurately, but it will also improve your overall emotional intelligence and interpersonal relationships.

Developing keen observation skills is crucial for accurately reading nonverbal cues. These skills allow individuals to pick up on subtle gestures, expressions, and body language, providing valuable insights into the emotions and intentions of others. By honing their ability to observe and interpret these nonverbal signals, individuals can enhance their communication skills, build stronger relationships, and navigate social interactions more effectively.

Observation skills are like a muscle that can be strengthened through practice. The more one observes people in various settings and pays attention to their behavior, the sharper their observation skills become. Noticing changes in posture, facial expressions, tone of voice, and gestures can provide valuable clues about a person's emotional state and mindset. By actively observing others, individuals can improve their ability to decode nonverbal cues accurately.

Enhanced observation skills lead to more accurate interpretations of nonverbal signals. When individuals pay close attention to the nonverbal cues of those around them, they can better understand unspoken messages and underlying emotions. This heightened awareness allows for more nuanced communication and the ability to respond appropriately to the needs and feelings of others. By sharpening their observation skills, individuals can become more empathetic and attuned to the subtleties of human behavior.

Observation is a powerful tool for improving emotional intelligence. By developing the ability to observe nonverbal cues effectively, individuals can gain valuable insights into the thoughts and feelings of others. This increased understanding enhances interpersonal relationships and fosters greater self-awareness and empathy. Through consistent observation practice in various settings, individuals can strengthen their emotional intelligence and become more adept at navigating complex social dynamics.

Practical Exercises to Enhance Observation Skills for Interpreting Nonverbal Cues

Now that we understand the importance of observation skills in interpreting nonverbal cues, let's delve into some practical exercises to enhance our ability to observe and interpret people's behavior.

1. **People-watching:** One effective way to sharpen observation skills is by engaging in people-watching exercises. Find a comfortable spot in a public setting, such as a park or café, and observe individuals around you. Pay attention to their body language, facial expressions, and gestures. Try to decipher what emotions they might be experiencing based on their nonverbal cues.

2. **Video Analysis:** Another useful exercise is to watch videos of people in various situations and analyze their nonverbal communication. Pause the video at different points and observe the subtle cues like eye movements, hand gestures, and posture. Practice interpreting these cues to better understand the emotions and intentions behind them.

3. **Role-Playing:** Engaging in role-playing scenarios can also help improve observation skills. Partner with a friend or family member and take turns playing different roles. Focus on observing each other's nonverbal cues during the interaction. This exercise can provide valuable insights into how body language affects communication.

4. **Self-Reflection:** Take some time for self-reflection after social interactions. Review recent conversations or encounters and try to recall the nonverbal cues the other person displays. Reflect on how you interpreted these cues and whether your understanding was accurate. This practice can help fine-tune your observation skills over time.

5. **Mirror Exercise:** Stand before a mirror and practice different facial expressions and body postures. Observe how these changes influence your own emotions and mood. This exercise can increase self-awareness and sensitivity to nonverbal signals in yourself and others.

6. **Group Dynamics:** Observe group interactions in social settings or meetings. Pay attention to how individuals within the group communicate nonverbally with each other. Notice who takes on leadership roles, who seems more passive, and how conflicts are expressed through body language. Understanding group dynamics enhances observation skills in diverse social contexts.

7. **Daily Journaling:** Keep a journal where you record observations of people's behavior throughout your day. Note any patterns in body language, facial expressions, or gestures across different individuals or situations. Regular journaling can help track progress in honing your

observation skills.

Incorporating these exercises into your routine can enhance your ability to effectively observe and interpret nonverbal cues. Remember that practice is key in improving your observation skills, leading to more accurate interpretations of the silent language that shapes human interactions.

Encouraging Observation Practice in Various Settings

Enhancing your observation skills goes beyond just understanding the basics; it requires consistent practice and exposure to different environments. You can effectively refine your ability to interpret nonverbal cues by actively observing people in various settings. Diversifying your observation practice will expose you to a wider range of behaviors, gestures, and expressions, making you more adept at deciphering subtle signals.

Immersing Yourself in Social Gatherings

One way to sharpen your observation skills is by immersing yourself in social gatherings. Whether it's a casual get-together with friends or a networking event, pay close attention to how people interact, their body language, and facial expressions. By actively observing social dynamics, you can gain valuable insights into human behavior and improve your ability to interpret nonverbal cues.

Observing in Professional Settings

Note how individuals communicate nonverbally in professional meetings, conferences, or the workplace cafeteria. Observe posture, eye contact, hand gestures, and facial expressions to understand the underlying messages. Practice interpreting these cues discreetly to enhance your observational skills gradually.

People-Watching in Public Places

Public spaces like parks, cafes, or shopping centers provide excellent opportunities for people-watching. Spend some time observing individuals from a distance and try to infer their emotions and intentions based on their nonverbal behavior. This exercise can help you become more attuned to subtle cues and improve your ability to read others accurately.

Practicing Observation with Different Age Groups

Interacting with individuals of different age groups can offer unique insights into nonverbal communication. Observe how children, teenagers, adults, and the elderly express themselves through body language and facial cues. Understanding how nonverbal signals vary across age groups can broaden your perspective and deepen your interpretive skills.

Utilizing Technology for Observation

In today's digital age, technology provides another avenue for honing your observation skills. Watch documentaries, movies, or online videos focusing on body language and nonverbal communication. Analyze how characters convey emotions through gestures and expressions to enhance your observational abilities.

Seeking Feedback and Reflection

After practicing observation in various settings, seek feedback from trusted individuals on your interpretations of nonverbal cues. Reflect on your observations and discuss them with others to gain different perspectives and refine your analytical skills. Constructive feedback can help you identify blind spots and improve your accuracy in reading nonverbal signals.

Incorporating these diverse practices into your routine can significantly enhance your observation skills. Remember that consistent effort and dedication are key to effectively mastering the art of interpreting nonverbal cues.

Developing keen observation skills is not just a useful tool but essential for mastering nonverbal communication. Focusing on this chapter's core concepts can transform how you perceive and interact with others. Observation is the foundation upon which all interpretation of human behavior is built. When you practice observing people in various settings, you begin to notice subtle changes and patterns that reveal their true feelings and intentions.

To make meaningful progress, engaging in the suggested exercises diligently is crucial. These activities enhance your ability to notice and interpret nonverbal cues more accurately. They are practical steps that can easily be incorporated into your daily routine, making them highly effective without requiring significant time or effort.

Consistency is key. Regularly practicing observation in different environments will steadily improve your skills. Whether you're at a café, in a meeting, or simply watching a movie, take a moment to focus on the nonverbal signals around you. This continuous practice sharpens your observational abilities and deepens your understanding of human behavior.

Remember, observation is an active skill that requires conscious effort and attention. The more you practice, the better you interpret the silent language of nonverbal communication. This capability will empower you to connect more deeply with others, navigate social situations more easily, and achieve higher emotional intelligence.

In summary, honing your observation skills is an achievable goal with immense benefits. By following the strategies outlined in this chapter and committing to regular practice, you can unlock new dimensions of understanding in your interactions with others. Embrace this journey towards enhanced perception and let it enrich every aspect of your personal and professional life.

Chapter 10: Gesture Speak: Interpreting the Body's Subtle Signals

"The art of communication is the art of hearing

as well as of being heard."

William Hazlitt

Can You Really Decode Emotions Through Gestures?

In our quest to understand human behavior, it's easy to overlook the silent language spoken by our bodies. Our words may be carefully chosen, but our body language often reveals our true feelings. This chapter dives deep into our bodies' subtle signals, offering you tools to interpret these cues accurately. By becoming proficient in reading body language, you can gain immediate insights into a person's emotional state or attitude during an interaction.

Understanding body language is not just about recognizing obvious signs like a smile or a frown. It's about becoming aware of the subtler indicators that often go unnoticed—like a fleeting glance, a slight shift in posture, or the position of someone's hands. These tiny gestures can speak volumes about what someone thinks or feels. For instance, crossed arms might indicate defensiveness, while an open posture suggests receptiveness and openness to dialogue.

Familiarizing yourself with these common indicators is the first step toward mastering nonverbal communication. Each gesture or posture conveys specific emotions or attitudes, and recognizing these can enhance your interactions significantly. This chapter will equip you with the knowledge and techniques to decode these signals effectively.

Next, we'll guide you on applying this awareness in real-life situations. Imagine gauging your colleague's enthusiasm for a project by observing their body language during a meeting. Or consider how useful it would be to sense your friend's discomfort even if they say they're fine. By actively looking for and interpreting these cues, you'll become more attuned to the unspoken messages around you.

Body language doesn't just reveal emotions; it also provides context to verbal communication. A person's words might say one thing, but their body could tell a different story altogether. Reading these signals can help you navigate social interactions more smoothly and respond empathetically.

Practical exercises and activities will also be part of your journey in this chapter. These will help you improve your ability to identify and interpret emotions through body language, making you more adept at responding appropriately in various social settings. From recognizing nervousness through fidgeting hands to understanding confidence through upright postures, each exercise will enhance your observational skills.

Finally, it's important to reflect on your interpretation accuracy and seek feedback from others. This continuous practice will refine your skills and build confidence in reading body language correctly. Remember, mastering this silent language is not just about observation; it's about empathy and a better understanding of the people around you.

Decoding Gestures: A Step-by-Step Guide

Step 1: Familiarize Yourself with Common Body Language Indicators

- **List Common Indicators:** Identify body language cues

such as hand gestures, facial expressions, postures, and movements.

- **Detail Each Indicator:** Explain what each indicator means and the emotions or attitudes they convey.
- **Visual Demonstrations:** Use illustrations or diagrams to provide clear examples of each indicator for better understanding.

Step 2: Apply Body Language Awareness Techniques in Real-Life Interactions

- **Observe and Interpret:** Actively observe people's body language in everyday situations.
- **Scenario Examples:** Provide specific scenarios where body language plays a crucial role.
- **Active Application:** Encourage readers to apply their understanding of body language cues during real-life interactions.

Step 3: Understand the Relationship Between Body Language and Emotions

- **Reveal Emotions:** Explain how different body language indicators reveal underlying emotions or attitudes.
- **Connect Indicators with Emotions:** Discuss how gestures like crossed arms indicate defensiveness or folded hands indicate nervousness.

- **Practice Activities:** Provide exercises for readers to practice identifying and interpreting emotions through body language.

Step 4: Practice Reading Body Language

- **Engaging Exercises:** Suggest exercises or games that allow readers to practice reading body language cues.
- **Interactive Resources:** Provide links to online videos or interactive quizzes that simulate real-life scenarios for practice.
- **Social Observation:** Encourage readers to observe body language in various social settings for improved skill development.

Step 5: Reflect on Interpretation Accuracy

- **Self-Evaluation:** Encourage readers to reflect on their interpretations of body language cues.
- **Seek Feedback:** Advice seeking feedback from others for improvement.
- **Continuous Learning:** Emphasize the importance of ongoing practice and learning for refining interpretation skills.

By following this structured process, you'll develop a keen eye for nonverbal communication and gain deeper insights into the silent messages conveyed by those around you.

Decoding the Silent Language: Understanding Body Language

Body language is a universal form of communication that often speaks louder than words. Understanding the subtle cues individuals exhibit through body movements can provide valuable insights into their thoughts, emotions, and attitudes. Familiarizing yourself with common body language indicators and their meanings can empower you to navigate social interactions more effectively and build stronger connections with others.

One of the most recognizable body language signals is crossed arms, which typically indicate defensiveness or closed-off behavior. On the contrary, an open posture with arms uncrossed suggests receptiveness and openness to communication. Eye contact is another crucial aspect of nonverbal communication. Sustained eye contact often indicates interest and attentiveness, while avoiding eye contact may signal discomfort or dishonesty.

Gestures such as nodding can convey agreement or understanding while shaking one's head may indicate disagreement or disbelief. Mirroring is a powerful technique where individuals subconsciously mimic each other's gestures, signaling rapport and connection. Paying attention to these subtle cues can help you establish a deeper understanding in your interactions with others.

Facial expressions play a significant role in conveying emotions and intentions. A genuine smile, characterized by crinkling around the eyes, signifies warmth and sincerity. Conversely, a forced smile that does not reach the eyes can be perceived as insincere. Microexpressions, fleeting facial expressions that reveal true emotions, are essential to accurately interpret someone's feelings.

Posture also communicates volumes about an individual's confidence and attitude. Standing tall with shoulders back exudes confidence and assertiveness, while slouching may indicate insecurity or low self-esteem. Gestures like handshakes can convey trust and respect when executed firmly but not overly so.

Understanding these common body language indicators equips you with valuable tools for deciphering the unspoken messages people convey daily. By honing your awareness of nonverbal cues, you can enhance your emotional intelligence and improve your relationships personally and professionally. Continue reading to learn how to apply body language awareness techniques in real-life interactions, gaining a deeper insight into our silent language.

Body language awareness techniques are theoretical concepts and practical tools that can significantly impact real-life interactions. By applying these techniques, individuals can navigate social situations more effectively and understand the unspoken messages conveyed by others. One key aspect of using body language awareness is observation. Paying attention to subtle cues such as facial expressions, gestures, and posture can provide valuable insights into a person's emotional state or intentions.

When interacting with others, it's essential to maintain open body language. This means avoiding crossing your arms, standing with a closed-off posture, or avoiding eye contact. Open body language signals receptiveness and approachability, encouraging positive communication and fostering trust between individuals. Additionally, mirroring the body language of the person you are engaging with can help create a sense of connection and rapport.

Another crucial aspect of applying body language awareness techniques is regulating nonverbal cues. Being mindful of your gestures, facial expressions, and tone of voice can ensure that your communication aligns with your intended message. For example, maintaining good eye contact conveys confidence and interest, while fidgeting or avoiding eye contact may signal discomfort or dishonesty.

Active listening plays a significant role in interpreting body language accurately. Focusing on verbal and nonverbal cues during a conversation, you can better understand the speaker's emotions and underlying messages. Remember that body language often reveals more than words alone, so being attentive to these cues can enhance your comprehension of the interaction.

Practice empathy in your interactions by considering the perspective of the other person. Try to put yourself in their shoes and understand their emotions and motivations. Empathy helps build trust and rapport, creating a more harmonious individual exchange. You demonstrate respect and understanding by acknowledging and validating the feelings expressed through body language.

Using body language awareness techniques in real-life interactions requires practice and patience. Start by observing the nonverbal cues of those around you in different situations. Notice patterns in how people express emotions through their gestures, facial expressions, and posture. Over time, you will become more adept at interpreting these signals accurately and responding appropriately.

Remember that body language is a universal form of communication, transcending cultural barriers and spoken language differences. You can significantly enhance your emotional intelligence and interpersonal skills by honing your ability to read and interpret nonverbal cues. The insights gained from applying body language awareness techniques can empower you to navigate social interactions with confidence and authenticity, leading to more meaningful connections with others.

In summary, applying body language awareness techniques involves keen observation, maintaining open body language, regulating nonverbal cues, active listening, practicing empathy, and consistent practice. By incorporating these strategies into your daily interactions, you can enhance your communication skills, build stronger relationships, and gain a deeper understanding of human behavior through the silent language of the body.

Body language can be a powerful tool for understanding the emotions and attitudes of others. We can gain valuable insights into their underlying feelings by observing subtle cues in how a person carries themselves, gestures, and facial expressions. Interpreting body language requires a keen eye and an understanding of common indicators, such as crossed arms indicating defensiveness or a relaxed posture suggesting openness. These cues can provide immediate clues about a person's emotional state during an interaction.

To master the art of reading body language effectively, paying attention to clusters of signals rather than isolated movements is crucial. For instance, a person might smile while crossing their arms, indicating a discrepancy between verbal and nonverbal communication. This inconsistency could signal discomfort or insincerity, prompting further exploration into the individual's feelings.

Gestures and body language are often more revealing than words, as they can betray hidden emotions that someone may be trying to conceal. Understanding these nonverbal cues allows us to navigate social interactions with greater empathy and sensitivity. By recognizing the unspoken messages conveyed through body language, we can respond appropriately and foster more authentic connections with others.

Facial expressions play a significant role in decoding emotions, often involuntary reactions reflecting our true feelings. A furrowed brow may indicate confusion or concern, while a genuine smile can signal happiness or approval. By honing our ability to interpret facial expressions, we can better understand the emotional landscape of those around us.

Posture and body movements also offer valuable insights into a person's mindset. Leaning in during a conversation can convey interest and engagement. At the same time, fidgeting or avoiding eye contact may suggest discomfort or unease. Being attuned to these subtleties enables us to adjust our behavior accordingly, fostering better communication and rapport with others.

In social and professional settings, the ability to read body language effectively can be a game-changer. It allows us to navigate complex interpersonal dynamics with confidence and insight, leading to more successful interactions and relationships. By sharpening our awareness of nonverbal cues, we can enhance our emotional intelligence and cultivate stronger connections with those around us.

Ultimately, mastering the skill of interpreting body language is about developing empathy and understanding. It involves being present at the moment and actively listening not just with our ears but also with our eyes. By immersing ourselves in the silent language of gestures and expressions, we can deepen our relationships, foster trust, and create meaningful connections that transcend words alone.

Body language is a universal form of communication that transcends cultural boundaries, offering valuable insights into human behavior across diverse contexts. By honing our ability to decipher these nonverbal cues, we equip ourselves with a powerful tool for navigating social interactions gracefully and insightfully. Embracing the subtleties of gesture speak allows us to connect more deeply with others, fostering genuine understanding and empathy in our interactions.

Mastering body language awareness is more than just an academic exercise; it's a practical skill that can transform how we interact with others. By familiarizing yourself with common body language indicators, you gain a powerful tool to decode the unspoken messages people convey. This knowledge equips you to navigate social situations with greater confidence and empathy.

Applying these techniques in real-life interactions doesn't require perfection but practice. Begin by observing others in everyday settings—notice how crossed arms might indicate defensiveness or how an open posture suggests receptiveness. Your ability to connect and communicate improves significantly as you become more attuned to these signals.

Moreover, understanding how body language reveals underlying emotions or attitudes allows for deeper emotional intelligence. When you recognize the subtle cues of discomfort, interest, or anxiety, you can respond more appropriately, fostering better relationships and smoother interactions.

Remember, the goal is not to become a mind reader but to enhance your awareness and responsiveness. With consistent practice, you'll find that interpreting body language becomes second nature, giving you invaluable insights into the silent language of human behavior. You have the innate ability to master these skills, empowering you to navigate your social world with greater ease and effectiveness.

Continue to observe, practice, and reflect on your interactions. Doing so will unlock new levels of understanding and connection with those around you.

Chapter 11: Faces Tell Tales: Unlocking Emotions through Facial Expressions

"Words – so innocent and powerless as they are, as standing

in a dictionary, how potent for good and evil they

become in the hands of one who knows

how to combine them."

Nathaniel Hawthorne

What Are Faces Really Saying?

Understanding the silent language of facial expressions is a pivotal skill in interpreting human behavior. Our faces are powerful communicators that convey emotions without uttering a word. Learning to decode these expressions is an academic exercise and a tool for enhancing emotional intelligence and building more profound connections with others. This chapter will guide you through the fundamentals of recognizing emotions through facial expressions, introduce you to systems like Ekman's Facial Action Coding System (FACS), and provide practical exercises to hone your skills.

Facial expressions are universal indicators of our internal emotional states. These micro-movements communicate volumes, whether a smile hinting at happiness or a furrowed brow indicating concern. Understanding these cues allows us to respond empathetically and effectively in social interactions. Recognizing basic emotions such as happiness, sadness, anger, fear, surprise, disgust, and contempt is crucial for anyone aiming to master nonverbal communication.

Paul Ekman's FACS offers a scientific approach to decoding facial expressions by analyzing muscle movements. This system breaks down facial expressions into specific action units (AUs), which correspond to particular muscle movements. By learning FACS, you gain a nuanced understanding of how different emotions manifest on the face, enabling you to identify even subtle changes that might go unnoticed.

Practice is key when it comes to mastering the interpretation of facial expressions. Engaging in exercises that challenge you to recognize and analyze various facial cues can significantly improve your emotional understanding. This practice enhances your ability to read others and sharpens your emotional awareness, leading to better interpersonal relationships.

Emotional connectivity stems from accurately interpreting others' feelings through their facial expressions. When you can discern what someone is feeling without them having to verbalize it, you build deeper trust and rapport. This skill is invaluable in personal and professional settings where empathy and understanding are paramount.

Feedback plays an essential role in refining your ability to read facial expressions. Seeking input from others about your interpretations can highlight areas for improvement and validate your progress. Continuous practice combined with constructive feedback ensures you become proficient in this silent yet potent form of communication.

The following sections will detail a step-by-step process for recognizing and interpreting facial expressions using FACS and other tools. By breaking down this complex skill into manageable steps, you'll be equipped with practical strategies for enhancing your emotional intelligence and connectivity.

Step-by-Step Process: Mastering the Silent Language

Objective: To develop the ability to accurately recognize and interpret basic emotions conveyed through facial expressions using structured tools like FACS.

Step 1: Learn the Basics of Recognizing Facial Expressions

- **Understand Major Categories:** Start by familiarizing yourself with the seven basic emotions: happiness, sadness, anger, fear, surprise, disgust, and contempt.
- **Manifestations on the Face:** Learn how each emotion typically appears on the face—happiness often shows as a smile with raised cheeks. At the same time, sadness might present as downturned lips and drooping eyelids.
- **Visual Examples:** Use visual aids or images showcasing these expressions to reinforce learning.

Step 2: Introduce Tools and Systems for Facial Expression Analysis

- **Ekman's FACS:** Dive into Paul Ekman's Facial Action Coding System (FACS), which categorizes muscle movements related to different emotions.
- **Nuanced Understanding:** Utilize resources like textbooks or online courses on FACS for an in-depth study.
- **Further Exploration:** Refer to recommended readings or websites that offer detailed insights into facial expression analysis.

Step 3: Practice Reading Facial Expressions

- **Exercises & Activities:** Engage in activities designed to test your recognition skills—watch videos or look at images where people display various emotions.
- **Analyze Features:** Analyze specific features like eye movements or mouth positions to determine underlying emotions.
- **Consistent Practice:** Regularly practice with diverse examples to build confidence and accuracy.

Step 4: Enhance Emotional Understanding and Connectivity

- **Significance in Relationships:** Recognize how interpreting facial cues can strengthen emotional bonds by fostering empathy.
- **Real-Life Application:** Apply these skills in daily interactions—notice how accurately reading someone's expression can change the dynamics of a conversation.
- **Empathy Development:** Use your enhanced understanding of emotions to respond empathetically and effectively.

Step 5: Seek Feedback and Further Develop Skills

- **Constructive Feedback:** Ask friends or colleagues for feedback on your interpretations of their facial expressions.

- **Additional Resources:** Continue learning through advanced courses or workshops on nonverbal communication.
- **Continuous Refinement:** Emphasize ongoing practice and adaptation based on feedback received.

Following this structured approach, you will become adept at reading facial expressions and enhance your overall emotional intelligence—a vital skill in today's interconnected world.

Understanding emotions through facial expressions is a fundamental aspect of human interaction. Faces tell tales, revealing many feelings that can sometimes be challenging to interpret accurately. Recognizing basic emotions conveyed through facial expressions is crucial for enhancing emotional intelligence and improving social interactions. By familiarizing oneself with common facial cues associated with various emotions, individuals can gain valuable insights into others' feelings and respond empathetically.

Facial expressions serve as windows to the soul, providing glimpses into the inner emotional states of individuals. From joy to sadness, anger to surprise, each emotion manifests uniquely on the face through muscle movements and subtle cues. By honing the ability to identify these distinct expressions, one can navigate social interactions more effectively and cultivate deeper connections.

Ekman's Facial Action Coding System (FACS) is a valuable tool that breaks down facial expressions into specific muscle movements, allowing for a detailed analysis of emotions displayed on the face. Understanding the intricacies of FACS can provide individuals with a comprehensive framework for interpreting facial cues accurately. By studying the muscle actions associated with different emotions, one can enhance one's ability to decipher subtle emotional signals in others' expressions.

Practicing the recognition of facial expressions is essential for honing this skill. Engaging in exercises that involve observing and identifying various emotions displayed by different individuals can help sharpen one's ability to read facial cues effectively. By actively seeking opportunities to practice recognizing emotions in real-life situations, individuals can improve their emotional understanding and develop greater empathy toward others.

Unlocking the Secrets Hidden in Facial Expressions

Facial expressions are powerful indicators of emotions, conveying much information about someone's feelings. Understanding these expressions goes beyond just recognizing a smile or a frown; it involves delving into the intricate details of muscle movements and microexpressions that can reveal subtle nuances of emotion. Ekman's Facial Action Coding System (FACS) provides a structured framework for analyzing facial expressions in detail, breaking down movements into specific action units that correspond to different emotions.

By familiarizing yourself with Ekman's FACS, you gain a deeper insight into the complexity of facial expressions. Each muscle movement on the face corresponds to a specific action unit, allowing for a more nuanced understanding of the emotions being displayed. This detailed analysis can help you pinpoint the primary emotion being expressed and any underlying or conflicting feelings that may be present.

Practicing with Ekman's FACS can enhance your ability to accurately interpret facial expressions in real-time situations. You can better understand their true emotional state by training yourself to recognize the subtle cues and microexpressions that flit across someone's face. This skill is invaluable in personal and professional settings, enabling you to respond appropriately to others' emotions and build stronger connections based on empathy and understanding.

The beauty of Ekman's FACS lies in its universal applicability across cultures. Emotions are expressed through facial expressions in remarkably similar ways worldwide, making this system a valuable tool for decoding nonverbal cues regardless of where you are. Whether interacting with someone from your own culture or bridging the gap with someone from a different background, Ekman's FACS provides a common language through which emotions can be understood and shared.

Engaging with Ekman's FACS sharpens your observational skills and deepens your emotional intelligence. As you become more attuned to the intricacies of facial expressions, you develop a heightened sensitivity to others' feelings and experiences. This increased emotional acuity fosters better communication, conflict resolution, and overall relationship building, empowering you to navigate social interactions with confidence and insight.

Incorporating Ekman's FACS into your daily practice can transform your engagement with the world around you. Honing your ability to read facial expressions accurately opens up new avenues for connection and understanding in your personal and professional relationships. Take the time to familiarize yourself with this powerful tool, and watch as your emotional intelligence flourishes, enriching every interaction with depth and authenticity.

The Emotional Decoding Process Model

The emotional decoding process model is designed to assist individuals in systematically reading and interpreting facial expressions. By drawing from Ekman's Facial Action Coding System (FACS) and simplifying it for everyday use, this framework guides readers through steps to identify facial movements, link them to specific emotions, understand the context, and respond appropriately.

Detection Phase:

The first step in the process involves **noticing subtle facial changes**. This phase requires keen observation skills to identify even the slightest shifts in expression. It is essential to pay attention to microexpressions that can convey underlying emotions that are not immediately obvious.

Identification Phase:

The identification phase focuses on recognizing specific muscle movements associated with different emotions. Individuals can more accurately decipher the feelings being expressed by learning to pinpoint these movements. Understanding the nuances of each expression helps distinguish between similar emotions.

Contextualization Phase:

In the contextualization phase, individuals consider the situation and other nonverbal cues. Understanding the context in which the emotion is displayed provides crucial insights into its authenticity and intensity. This step helps in avoiding misinterpretations based solely on facial expressions.

Response Phase:

The final step involves deciding on an appropriate reaction based on the perceived emotion. This phase requires individuals to apply their understanding of facial expressions to formulate suitable responses. Responding empathetically and effectively can enhance communication and foster better relationships.

The components of this model interact harmoniously, with each phase building upon the previous one to facilitate a comprehensive understanding of facial expressions and emotions.

Practical Implications:

By following this process model, individuals can enhance their emotional intelligence, improve their ability to connect with others and communicate more effectively. Understanding facial expressions aids in building trust, resolving conflicts, and fostering empathy. The practical implications of this model extend beyond personal interactions into professional settings where emotional intelligence plays a crucial role in leadership and teamwork.

In summary, the emotional decoding process model provides a structured approach to interpreting facial expressions, enabling individuals to navigate social interactions with greater insight and empathy. By honing these skills, readers can deepen their emotional understanding and forge stronger connections with those around them.

Recognizing facial expressions is more than just identifying a smile or a frown. It's about understanding the intricate dance of muscle movements that convey our deepest emotions. Mastering this skill can significantly enhance your ability to connect profoundly with others.

By now, you should have a solid foundation in recognizing the basics of facial expressions. This isn't just academic knowledge; it's a practical tool you can use daily. The detailed insights provided by Ekman's Facial Action Coding System (FACS) offer a structured way to decode even the subtlest emotions, making your interpretations more accurate and reliable.

Practicing these skills is essential. Just like any other ability, proficiency comes with repetition and conscious effort. Make it a habit to observe the faces around you—whether in conversations, while watching media, or even in photographs. This ongoing practice will sharpen your awareness and improve your emotional intelligence.

Remember, this journey isn't about achieving perfection but enhancing your understanding and empathy towards others. Every step in learning to read facial expressions brings you closer to truly seeing and connecting with those around you.

Take control of this learning process. Your capacity for emotional mastery is within reach, and with diligent practice, the benefits will be substantial. Improved relationships, better communication, and a deeper sense of empathy are all within your grasp.

As we move forward, keep building on these foundational skills. The knowledge you've gained here will serve as a cornerstone for further developing your nonverbal communication abilities. You have the tools—now it's time to put them into action.

Chapter 12: Practice Makes Perfect: Reinforcing Skills through Real-life Applications

"Listening is being able to be changed

by the other person."

Alan Alda

Discover the Power of Practice in Mastering Nonverbal Communication

When it comes to mastering nonverbal communication, theory

alone isn't enough. Understanding the principles of body language and emotional cues is essential, but these insights can quickly fade without practical application. This chapter delves into the necessity of reinforcing skills through hands-on exercises, ensuring that readers not only learn but retain and refine their ability to interpret the silent language of human behavior.

Engaging in practical exercises is a cornerstone for skill reinforcement. Mirroring nonverbal cues, for instance, is a powerful method to deepen your understanding of body language. By consciously mimicking the gestures, posture, and facial expressions of others, you start to internalize these signals, making it easier to recognize and interpret them in real-life interactions. It's not about imitation for flattery; it's about internalizing the nuances of nonverbal communication.

Another effective exercise involves interpreting emotions in silent video clips. Stripped of dialogue, these clips compel you to focus solely on facial expressions, body movements, and other nonverbal cues to understand the underlying emotions and intentions. This practice sharpens your observational skills and enhances your ability to read people accurately in everyday situations. When you practice consistently, you develop a keen sense of detecting subtleties that might go unnoticed.

But why are these exercises so crucial? Continuous practice ensures that your skills are honed and retained over time. Just like any other skill—whether playing an instrument or learning a new language—regular practice cements your abilities and makes them second nature. Even the most insightful knowledge can become rusty and less effective without consistent reinforcement.

Integrate these exercises into your daily routine to make this process engaging and manageable. For example, mute the sound periodically while watching TV or a movie and try to infer what's happening based solely on visual cues. Or, during social gatherings, take mental notes on people's body language and later reflect on what those signals might have conveyed. These small yet intentional practices can significantly bolster your proficiency over time.

Practical application isn't just about individual exercises; it's also about fostering a mindset geared towards continuous improvement. Approach each interaction as an opportunity to apply what you've learned. Be mindful of your own nonverbal signals as well as those of others. Reflect on your experiences—what did you notice? How did it align with what you've studied? What could you do differently next time?

Lastly, remember that mastery in nonverbal communication is a journey rather than a destination. The more you practice, the more intuitive these skills will become. Embrace each mistake as a learning opportunity rather than a setback. Celebrate small victories when you successfully interpret someone's unspoken feelings or intentions.

By incorporating these practical exercises into your routine and maintaining a commitment to continuous practice, you'll find that interpreting nonverbal cues becomes second nature over time. This chapter provides insights and actionable strategies to ensure you're equipped with the tools to master reading human behavior's silent language.

Practical exercises are essential to reinforce and enhance your nonverbal communication skills. These exercises serve as opportunities to put theory into practice, allowing you to develop a deeper understanding of body language and facial expressions. By engaging in real-life scenarios, you can fine-tune your ability to interpret nonverbal cues accurately. Practice is key to mastering any skill, and nonverbal communication is no exception.

One practical exercise involves observing people in various social settings without engaging in conversation. Take note of their body language, facial expressions, and gestures. Try to decipher the underlying emotions or intentions behind their nonverbal cues. This exercise helps sharpen your observational skills and enhances your ability to read nonverbal signals accurately.

Another effective exercise is mirroring nonverbal cues during interactions. Practice reflecting the body language of others to establish rapport and build connections. This technique improves your ability to interpret nonverbal signals and enhances your nonverbal communication skills. You can create a sense of understanding and harmony in social interactions by mirroring gestures, posture, and expressions.

Interpreting emotions in silent video clips is valuable for honing your nonverbal communication skills. Watch videos without sound and focus on deciphering emotions through facial expressions and body language. Pay attention to subtle cues such as microexpressions, eye movements, and hand gestures. This exercise trains your ability to pick up on nuanced nonverbal signals, improving your emotional intelligence.

Engaging in role-playing scenarios is an interactive way to reinforce your understanding of nonverbal communication. Act out different social situations with a partner and pay close attention to each other's body language and gestures. By embodying various roles, you can experience firsthand how nonverbal cues influence interactions and practice adjusting your own signals accordingly.

Mastering Nonverbal Communication: The Power of Practice

Interpreting emotions and intentions in silent video clips or live interactions requires a keen eye for detail and a deep understanding of nonverbal cues. When watching silent video clips, focus on facial expressions, body language, and tone of voice to decipher the underlying emotions. Pay attention to micro-expressions, subtle movements that can reveal true feelings. Practice mirroring these expressions yourself to understand their impact on communication.

In live interactions, observe how people hold themselves, their gestures, and how they make eye contact. Look for congruence between verbal and nonverbal cues to gain insight into someone's true feelings. Remember that nonverbal cues often convey emotions more accurately than words do. Practice active listening to identify subtle cues that may indicate underlying emotions.

To interpret emotions effectively, put yourself in the other person's shoes. Consider their perspective, background, and current situation to better understand their emotional state. Ask open-ended questions to encourage them to express themselves verbally, complementing the nonverbal signals they are sending.

When analyzing silent video clips, pause and rewind to focus on specific gestures or expressions. Take note of recurring patterns in body language or facial expressions that can help you decode emotions more efficiently in future interactions. Engage in role-playing exercises to practice interpreting emotions in different scenarios, enhancing your ability to read nonverbal cues accurately.

In live interactions, maintain a curious mindset and be open to learning from each encounter. Reflect on your observations afterward to identify areas for improvement and further understanding. Seek feedback from trusted peers or mentors to gain additional insights into interpreting emotions effectively.

Remember that interpreting emotions is a skill that improves with practice and dedication. Consistent exposure to real-life situations where nonverbal cues play a significant role will sharpen your abilities over time. Embrace each interaction as an opportunity to hone your skills and deepen your understanding of human behavior through nonverbal communication.

Continuous practice is the key to improving and retaining nonverbal communication skills. Repetition of practical exercises, such as mirroring nonverbal cues and interpreting emotions in silent video clips, is essential for skill enhancement. By engaging regularly in these hands-on activities, individuals can strengthen their proficiency in reading nonverbal signals and become more adept at navigating social interactions.

Consistent practice ensures that the skills learned are honed and retained over time. Just like any other skill, mastering nonverbal communication requires dedication and effort. Through repeated exposure to real-life scenarios and practical exercises, individuals can internalize the knowledge gained from this book and apply it effectively in their daily interactions.

This chapter encourages readers to commit to ongoing improvement by emphasizing the importance of continuous practice. It is not enough to learn about nonverbal cues once; one must actively engage with the material and put it into practice regularly. Through repeated application of the strategies and techniques outlined in this book, individuals can solidify their understanding of nonverbal communication and develop a heightened sense of emotional intelligence.

Reinforcement through practice allows individuals to fine-tune their ability to interpret emotions accurately and respond appropriately in various social contexts. The more one practices decoding nonverbal signals, the more intuitive it becomes. With each practical exercise completed, individuals are one step closer to mastering the silent language of human behavior.

The message is clear: practice makes perfect for honing nonverbal communication skills. By engaging consistently in practical exercises, individuals can reinforce their learning, improve their proficiency in reading nonverbal cues, and enhance their ability to authentically connect with others. Continuous practice is not just a recommendation but a critical component in mastering the art of interpreting nonverbal signals.

Mastering nonverbal communication and emotional intelligence requires more than just understanding concepts; it demands consistent practice and real-life application. By engaging in the practical exercises provided, such as mirroring nonverbal cues and interpreting emotions in silent video clips, you are taking crucial steps to solidify your learning. These hands-on activities allow you to see immediate results, reinforcing your confidence in reading nonverbal signals accurately.

Continuous practice is key. Like any other skill, the more you practice, the better you become. Consistency sharpens your abilities and ensures that these skills become second nature. Whether observing silent video clips or interacting with people in your daily life, each opportunity to practice brings you closer to mastering the silent language of human behavior.

Remember, interpreting emotions and intentions accurately is not an innate talent but a cultivated skill. Applying the suggested strategies regularly will enhance your ability to understand others deeply and respond appropriately. This improved understanding fosters stronger relationships and more effective communication in both personal and professional settings.

You have the power to take control of your progress. Embrace each exercise with intention and curiosity. Trust that every effort you put into practicing these techniques will yield tangible results. The journey to mastering nonverbal communication is ongoing, but with dedication and perseverance, you will continually improve.

In this chapter, we've provided actionable advice designed for easy implementation. Now, it's up to you to apply these strategies consistently. By doing so, you'll not only reinforce what you've learned but also retain these invaluable skills for years to come.

Stay committed to practicing regularly, and remember that every interaction is an opportunity for growth. With each step forward, you're becoming more adept at reading the silent language of human behavior—unlocking a deeper understanding of those around you and enhancing your emotional intelligence in profound ways.

Chapter 13: The Journey Never Ends: Embracing Lifelong Learning in Nonverbal Communication

"The greatest problem with communication is we don't listen to understand. We listen to reply."

Roy T. Bennett

Discover the Unending Path to Mastery in Nonverbal Communication

In an ever-evolving world, the pursuit of understanding human behavior through nonverbal communication is not a one-time achievement but a continuous journey. The silent language of gestures, expressions, and body movements holds immense power, profoundly shaping personal and professional interactions. As you delve deeper into this chapter, you will realize that committing to lifelong learning in nonverbal communication is essential for staying adept at interpreting these subtle cues.

The importance of this commitment cannot be overstated. Engaging with recommended resources like books, articles, and online courses ensures you remain updated with the latest insights and techniques. Authors and researchers frequently uncover new dimensions of nonverbal communication, making it crucial for you to stay informed. You can refine your understanding and application of nonverbal cues by consistently seeking new knowledge.

Consider the wealth of information available at your fingertips. Books such as "The Definitive Book of Body Language" by Allan and Barbara Pease or "What Every BODY is Saying" by Joe Navarro offer foundational knowledge and advanced strategies for reading nonverbal cues. Subscribing to academic journals or following experts on social media can also provide fresh perspectives and recent studies that enhance your skills.

Engage and Reflect: The Power of Discussion

To truly master nonverbal communication, practicing regularly and seeking feedback is vital. Discussions with peers or mentors allow for shared learning experiences where different interpretations can be explored. This collaborative approach solidifies your understanding and exposes you to diverse viewpoints that can broaden your perspective.

Feedback is an invaluable tool in this process. By inviting others to observe and comment on your interpretations, you gain insights into areas where you need improvement. Regular practice sessions with trusted colleagues or friends can help simulate real-world scenarios where nonverbal communication is critical. Through these interactions, your ability to read people accurately becomes more nuanced.

Lifelong Learning: A Gateway to Stronger Relationships

Commitment to lifelong learning in nonverbal communication extends beyond professional benefits; it significantly enhances personal relationships. Understanding the unspoken signals from loved ones fosters deeper connections and empathy. Recognizing subtle signs of discomfort or joy allows for more meaningful interactions, strengthening bonds over time.

In professional settings, being adept at reading nonverbal cues can set you apart as a leader who truly understands your team's needs and emotions. This skill fosters a positive work environment where employees feel seen and valued. Moreover, it enhances negotiation tactics, conflict resolution abilities, and interpersonal effectiveness.

Practical Steps Towards Mastery

To embark on this journey effectively, start by setting specific learning goals related to nonverbal communication. Identify key areas you wish to improve, whether recognizing micro-expressions or understanding cultural differences in body language. Seek out resources that cater specifically to these goals.

Allocate regular time for study and practice within your routine. Just as athletes train consistently to maintain peak performance, so should you dedicate time to honing your skills in nonverbal communication. Use online courses like Coursera or Udemy, which provide structured learning paths tailored to various aspects of body language interpretation.

Reaping the Rewards

The benefits of committing to lifelong learning in nonverbal communication are manifold. Enhanced personal relationships increase emotional satisfaction, while improved professional interactions contribute to career success. As you become more proficient in reading people's silent language, you'll find yourself navigating social landscapes confidently and easily.

By embracing continuous learning, discussing insights with others, and practicing regularly, you're not just improving a skill—you're transforming how you interact with the world around you. This commitment ensures you're always equipped with the latest knowledge and techniques for interpreting human behavior effectively.

Your journey in mastering nonverbal communication is indeed never-ending but profoundly rewarding. Each step forward opens new avenues for understanding others deeply while enhancing every interaction's quality, both personally and professionally. So, embark on this path enthusiastically, knowing that every effort made towards learning will bring lasting value into your life.

Continuous learning is vital to mastering the intricate world of nonverbal communication. As you progress on your journey to decode the silent language, you must seek resources to enhance your understanding and practical skills in this field. Books, articles, and online courses tailored to nonverbal communication can serve as invaluable tools in expanding your knowledge and refining your ability to interpret gestures, expressions, and body language.

Books are a timeless source of wisdom and insight. Look for titles authored by experts in nonverbal communication, such as Joe Navarro or Vanessa Van Edwards. These books often provide in-depth explanations of various nonverbal cues, real-life examples, and practical tips on how to apply this knowledge in everyday interactions. Consider starting with classics like "What Everybody is Saying" by Joe Navarro for a foundational understanding of body language.

Articles offer quick and digestible information that can keep you updated on the latest trends and research findings in nonverbal communication. Follow reputable websites, journals, and blogs on psychology, communication, or body language analysis. Reading articles regularly can help you stay informed about new studies, emerging theories, and innovative techniques for reading nonverbal cues effectively.

Online courses provide a structured learning environment that allows you to deepen your expertise at your own pace. Platforms like Coursera, Udemy, or LinkedIn Learning offer courses to improve nonverbal communication skills. These courses often include video lectures, interactive quizzes, and practical exercises that simulate real-world scenarios to enhance your ability to accurately interpret and respond to nonverbal cues.

By engaging with these resources consistently, you can expand your knowledge base, refine your observational skills, and develop a nuanced understanding of nonverbal communication. Remember that learning is a continuous process, and each book read or course completed brings you closer to becoming proficient in deciphering the silent language of human behavior.

Cultivating Nonverbal Communication Skills Through Discussion and Feedback

Engaging in discussions and seeking feedback from others is a valuable practice to refine nonverbal reading skills. By actively participating in conversations about body language and facial expressions, individuals can gain different perspectives and insights that contribute to their understanding of human behavior.

Sharing observations and interpretations with others creates a collaborative learning environment where feedback can be exchanged, allowing for mutual growth in nonverbal communication proficiency.

Practicing feedback is essential for honing one's ability to read people accurately. Receiving constructive criticism from peers or mentors helps individuals identify blind spots and areas for improvement in their nonverbal communication skills. Constructive feedback is a mirror that reflects how others perceive our body language, enabling us to make necessary adjustments to convey messages more effectively.

Engaging in discussions about nonverbal communication provides an opportunity to learn from others. It fosters a sense of community and support. Sharing experiences, challenges, and successes with like-minded individuals creates a supportive network where individuals can encourage each other's growth in interpreting nonverbal cues. Building connections with others committed to enhancing their nonverbal communication skills can motivate and inspire.

Practicing feedback in a safe and constructive environment allows individuals to experiment with different approaches to reading nonverbal cues without fear of judgment. Receiving feedback on our interpretations helps us refine our analytical skills and develop a more nuanced understanding of human behavior. Embracing feedback as a tool for growth rather than criticism empowers individuals to continuously improve their ability to decode nonverbal signals accurately.

Individuals create an environment conducive to continuous learning and improvement in nonverbal communication skills by engaging in discussions and seeking feedback from others. Active participation in these exchanges fosters a culture of openness, curiosity, and collaboration that supports ongoing personal development. Embracing discussing and practicing feedback with peers is a powerful way to refine one's ability to read people effectively.

Continuously engaging in learning opportunities related to nonverbal communication offers many benefits for personal and professional relationships. By committing to lifelong learning in this field, individuals can enhance their understanding of human behavior, improve their communication skills, and deepen their emotional intelligence. Understanding the intricacies of nonverbal cues can lead to more authentic connections with others, fostering stronger relationships built on trust and empathy.

One of the key advantages of ongoing learning in nonverbal communication is the ability to adapt to evolving social dynamics. As society changes and communication methods evolve, staying informed about the latest research and insights can help individuals navigate new challenges effectively. By continuously expanding their knowledge base, individuals can remain agile in interpreting nonverbal cues in various contexts, ensuring they are equipped to handle diverse interpersonal interactions.

Moreover, a commitment to lifelong learning in nonverbal communication can improve conflict resolution skills. By honing their ability to read body language, facial expressions, and other nonverbal signals, individuals can better understand and address the emotions underlying conflicts constructively. This enhanced insight can facilitate more effective communication during disagreements, leading to quicker resolutions and stronger relationships in both personal and professional settings.

Another significant benefit of ongoing learning in nonverbal communication is the development of empathy and compassion. By delving deeper into the nuances of human behavior, individuals can cultivate a greater sense of empathy towards others. Understanding the unspoken messages conveyed through nonverbal cues allows individuals to connect on a deeper level with those around them, fostering genuine relationships based on mutual understanding and respect.

Continuous learning in nonverbal communication also contributes to improved leadership skills. Leaders with a strong grasp of nonverbal cues can inspire trust and confidence in their teams by effectively conveying their messages verbally and nonverbally. By refining their ability to interpret body language and emotional expressions, leaders can create a more inclusive and supportive work environment, enhancing team morale and productivity.

Furthermore, lifelong learning in nonverbal communication can positively impact personal well-being. Individuals can cultivate self-awareness and emotional resilience by developing a deeper understanding of human behavior and emotions. This heightened self-awareness can lead to better self-regulation and improved mental health, enabling individuals to navigate challenging situations with greater composure and clarity.

In essence, embracing lifelong learning in nonverbal communication is not just about decoding gestures or expressions but about fostering meaningful connections with others based on empathy, understanding, and authenticity. By continually expanding their knowledge base in this area, individuals can enrich their personal relationships, advance their careers, and lead more fulfilling lives grounded in effective communication and emotional intelligence.

The journey of mastering nonverbal communication extends far beyond the confines of this book. Continuous learning is not just a recommendation; it's necessary for anyone serious about enhancing their ability to read and interpret human behavior. You ensure your knowledge remains current and comprehensive by engaging with the resources available—books, articles, and online courses. This commitment to ongoing education will sharpen your skills, making you more adept at navigating the silent language of nonverbal cues.

Equally important is engaging in discussions and seeking feedback from others. Dialogue with peers can provide fresh perspectives and insights that solitary study might miss. Regular practice and constructive criticism are invaluable for refining your nonverbal reading abilities. Consider forming study groups or joining forums where you can discuss concepts and share experiences. Teaching or explaining what you've learned to others can also solidify your understanding.

A commitment to lifelong learning in nonverbal communication yields profound benefits in both personal and professional realms. Enhanced nonverbal skills lead to more meaningful interactions, fostering deeper connections and improving relationships. In professional settings, being attuned to nonverbal signals can give you a competitive edge, making you more effective in negotiations, leadership, and team collaboration.

Remember, this journey is not about reaching a final destination but about continual growth and improvement. Every new book read, every conversation had, and every bit of feedback received adds another layer to your understanding. Your dedication to this path demonstrates a proactive approach to personal development. This trait will serve you well in all areas of life.

Take control of your learning journey by actively seeking opportunities to expand your knowledge and practice your skills. You have the innate ability to master emotional intelligence and overcome challenges through persistent effort and curiosity. Embrace this journey with enthusiasm and an open mind, knowing that each step forward enriches your comprehension of others and connection with the world around you.

In this ongoing pursuit, you are never alone. Countless resources and communities are available to support you as you develop your nonverbal communication skills. Your commitment to lifelong learning will unlock the secrets of human behavior and empower you to build stronger, more empathetic relationships throughout your life.

As we delve into the final chapter, keep these principles at heart: remain curious, stay engaged, and continually seek growth in understanding the silent language that connects us all.

Chapter 14: Bridging Worlds: Cultural Sensitivity in Nonverbal Communication

"Immature love says: 'I love you because I need you.'

Mature love says, 'I need you because I love you.'"

Erich Fromm

Unlocking Cross-Cultural Connections through Nonverbal Communication

Understanding nonverbal communication has never been more critical in a world where diverse cultures intersect daily. This chapter delves into the nuances of nonverbal cues across various cultures and the significance of cultural sensitivity in interpreting these signals accurately. Misinterpretations can lead to unintended offenses and misunderstandings, which can strain personal and professional relationships. Enhancing your awareness of cultural differences in nonverbal communication can foster more inclusive interactions and avoid common pitfalls.

The journey through this book has equipped you with a deep understanding of human behavior and nonverbal communication. You have learned to decode facial expressions, read body language, and grasp the underlying psychological mechanisms driving human interactions. Now, it's time to apply these insights on a global scale. Cultural sensitivity is not just about recognizing different norms but also about respecting them. This chapter will guide you in appreciating these differences and using this knowledge to improve interactions with people from diverse backgrounds.

Accurate interpretation of nonverbal cues is essential in multicultural settings. For instance, a gesture as simple as a nod can have different meanings across cultures—affirmative in some and dismissive in others. Understanding these variations helps prevent miscommunication and fosters better relationships. Learning about these nuances enriches your ability to read people accurately, ensuring that your interactions are respectful and effective.

Learning nonverbal communication norms from various cultures involves more than memorizing gestures; it requires immersing yourself in their context. This chapter will provide practical strategies to help you understand and adopt these norms. Whether observing interactions, engaging with diverse communities, or studying cultural etiquette, becoming culturally aware is an ongoing process that enhances your emotional intelligence.

By fostering inclusive interactions, you show respect for others and create an environment where everyone feels valued. This chapter will offer actionable advice on communicating inclusively through nonverbal cues. Simple adjustments like maintaining appropriate eye contact, respecting personal space, and being mindful of touch can significantly affect how your message is received.

Avoiding cultural misunderstandings is crucial for building trust and rapport in any setting. Through enhanced cultural awareness, you can navigate conversations with confidence and empathy. This chapter emphasizes the importance of being proactive rather than reactive—taking the initiative to learn about others' cultural backgrounds demonstrates genuine interest and respect.

Throughout this book, you've explored the silent language that shapes human behavior. By integrating cultural sensitivity into your understanding of nonverbal communication, you are better prepared to interact harmoniously with people from all walks of life. Your ability to interpret subtle cues accurately will enhance your interpersonal relationships and contribute positively to any social or professional scenario you encounter.

As we conclude this exploration of human behavior and nonverbal communication, remember that mastering these skills is an ongoing journey. The insights gained here serve as a foundation for continuous learning and growth. With compassion, awareness, and respect at the forefront, you're now equipped to bridge worlds through thoughtful and sensitive communication practices.

Cultural sensitivity is crucial to accurately interpreting nonverbal cues across different backgrounds. Understanding the variations in body language, facial expressions, and gestures among diverse cultures can prevent misunderstandings and misinterpretations. It is essential to recognize that what may be considered a positive gesture in one culture could be perceived differently in another. Cultivating cultural sensitivity allows individuals to navigate social interactions more effectively and build stronger connections with people from various backgrounds.

Misunderstandings often arise when individuals fail to consider the cultural context in which nonverbal communication occurs. A simple gesture or facial expression that seems harmless in one culture may carry a vastly different meaning in another. This lack of awareness can lead to unintended offense or confusion, hindering effective communication and relationship-building. By understanding different cultures' nonverbal norms, individuals can bridge these communication gaps and foster more meaningful interactions.

Cultural sensitivity extends beyond recognizing differences; it also involves embracing diversity and valuing the unique perspectives that each culture brings. By approaching interactions with an open mind and a willingness to learn, individuals can cultivate empathy and respect for others' ways of expressing themselves nonverbally. This enriches personal relationships and enhances professional collaborations by promoting inclusivity and understanding.

Learning about nonverbal communication norms in various cultures is an ongoing process that requires curiosity, observation, and a genuine interest in connecting with others authentically. By expanding one's cultural awareness and knowledge of nonverbal cues, individuals can navigate cross-cultural interactions more confidently and sensitively. Embracing cultural diversity enriches communication skills and deepens understanding of human behavior across different social contexts.

Nurturing Cultural Awareness in Nonverbal Communication

The journey towards enhancing cultural awareness begins with acknowledging the importance of respecting diverse expressions of body language, gestures, and facial cues. By valuing these differences and actively seeking to understand them, individuals can create harmonious relationships built on mutual respect and appreciation for cultural diversity.

Learning and understanding nonverbal communication norms in various cultures is crucial to fostering inclusive interactions and avoiding misunderstandings. Each culture has its own nonverbal cues and gestures that hold specific meanings, often differing from what one might be familiar with. By delving into the nuances of nonverbal communication across different cultural backgrounds, individuals can enhance their cross-cultural communication skills and build stronger connections with people from diverse origins.

One key aspect to consider when learning about nonverbal communication in different cultures is the significance of body language. In some cultures, maintaining eye contact shows respect and attentiveness. In contrast, it may be viewed as confrontational or disrespectful to others. Understanding these variations can prevent unintended offense and facilitate smoother interactions. Similarly, gestures like handshakes, bowing, or kissing on the cheek carry distinct meanings across cultures and should be approached with sensitivity and awareness.

Facial expressions also play a vital role in nonverbal communication, conveying emotions and intentions without words. However, the interpretation of facial expressions can vary widely between cultures. For example, a smile may signify happiness in one culture but conceal discomfort or unease in another. By familiarizing oneself with the cultural norms surrounding facial expressions, individuals can avoid misinterpretations and establish genuine connections based on mutual understanding.

Proxemics, or the use of personal space, differs among cultures and influences communication dynamics significantly. Some cultures prefer closer physical proximity during conversations, while others value more personal space. Being mindful of these differences can help individuals navigate social interactions respectfully and adapt their communication style to align with cultural preferences.

Gestures and body movements also hold cultural significance, with certain actions carrying specific meanings that may not be universal. For instance, a thumbs-up gesture may symbolize approval in one culture but be considered offensive in another. By learning about these cultural nuances, individuals can communicate effectively and avoid inadvertently causing offense or confusion.

To deepen understanding of nonverbal communication norms in various cultures, engaging in cultural immersion experiences is beneficial whenever possible. By interacting directly with individuals from different cultural backgrounds, observing their nonverbal behaviors, and seeking clarification when unsure, individuals can gain firsthand insights into the subtleties of cross-cultural communication.

In summary, cultivating an awareness of nonverbal communication norms across diverse cultures enhances one's ability to connect authentically with individuals from different backgrounds. By acknowledging and respecting these differences, individuals can navigate social interactions with sensitivity and cultural competence, fostering meaningful relationships built on mutual understanding and respect.

Cultural awareness plays a vital role in fostering inclusive interactions and avoiding misunderstandings in nonverbal communication. Enhancing our understanding of different cultural norms allows us to navigate diverse social settings more easily and sensitively. To foster inclusivity and avoid cultural faux pas, it is crucial to approach interactions with an open mind and a willingness to learn about the nonverbal cues specific to each culture.

One practical strategy for enhancing cultural awareness is to engage in active listening and observation when interacting with individuals from different cultural backgrounds. We can gain valuable insights into their communication style and preferences by paying close attention to their nonverbal cues, such as body language, facial expressions, and gestures. This heightened awareness allows us to adapt our nonverbal behavior accordingly, ensuring respectful and culturally sensitive interactions.

Another effective approach is to seek resources that provide information on nonverbal communication norms in various cultures. Books, online articles, and cultural sensitivity training programs can offer valuable insights into the unique ways different cultures express emotions, convey respect, and communicate nonverbally. By educating ourselves on these cultural nuances, we can avoid misinterpretations and misunderstandings arising from differences in nonverbal communication styles.

It is essential to approach cross-cultural interactions with curiosity and humility. By acknowledging that our own cultural perspectives may differ from those of others, we can create a space for open dialogue and mutual understanding. We can bridge cultural divides and build connections based on respect and empathy through active engagement and a willingness to learn.

Practicing empathy is key to fostering inclusive interactions across cultures. By putting ourselves in the shoes of others, we can better understand their perspectives and respond sensitively to their nonverbal cues. Empathy enables us to connect deeper, transcending cultural differences and fostering meaningful relationships based on mutual respect and understanding.

In conclusion, enhancing cultural awareness is essential for navigating the complexities of nonverbal communication across diverse cultural backgrounds. By approaching interactions with an open mind, actively listening, seeking out resources, practicing empathy, and adapting our behavior accordingly, we can foster inclusivity, avoid misunderstandings, and build connections based on mutual respect. Embracing cultural sensitivity enriches our ability to engage authentically with individuals from all walks of life, creating a more harmonious and interconnected global community.

Reflecting on our exploration of cultural sensitivity in nonverbal communication, it becomes evident that enhancing our awareness of cultural differences is beneficial and essential. Misinterpreting nonverbal cues can lead to misunderstandings, creating barriers in both personal and professional interactions. By dedicating time to learning and understanding the norms of various cultures, we open ourselves up to more inclusive and empathetic communication.

The journey through this book has equipped you with a comprehensive toolkit for decoding human behavior. From recognizing subtle facial expressions to interpreting body language, you now possess the skills to navigate the complex landscape of nonverbal communication with greater confidence and accuracy. These practical and transformative insights offer a pathway to more meaningful connections.

Cultivating emotional intelligence has been a recurring theme throughout our discussions. By honing this skill, you can better understand and manage your own emotions while also being attuned to the feelings of others. This dual awareness fosters stronger interpersonal relationships and enhances your ability to respond thoughtfully in various social scenarios.

It's crucial to remember that cultural sensitivity is a continuous learning process. As you interact with people from diverse backgrounds, remain curious and open-minded. Ask questions, observe carefully, and approach differences respectfully and with humility. This attitude will help you avoid cultural faux pas and enrich your understanding of the world around you.

By integrating these strategies into your daily life, you'll find that effective communication transcends words. Nonverbal cues provide a silent yet powerful language that, when understood correctly, can bridge gaps and build bridges between individuals from different walks of life.

Your journey doesn't end here. Continue to apply what you've learned, actively engage with new experiences, and refine your skills over time. The ability to interpret the silent language of human behavior is a dynamic process that will continually evolve as you grow and encounter new situations.

In closing, take pride in the progress you've made. You've embarked on mastering nonverbal communication and emotional intelligence. This journey promises lasting benefits for your personal growth and professional success. Embrace this newfound knowledge with confidence, knowing you are now better equipped to navigate the complexities of human interaction with empathy, insight, and respect.

Epilogue

"You never really understand a person until you

consider things from his point of view."

Harper Lee

Embracing the Silent Dialogue: A Journey Toward Understanding and Connection

As we conclude this journey, reflecting on the profound impact of mastering nonverbal communication and emotional intelligence on every facet of your life is important. From professional interactions to personal relationships, interpreting and responding to unspoken signals is invaluable. This book aims to equip you with the tools to navigate these complex waters confidently and empathetically.

Understanding human behavior through nonverbal cues is more than an academic exercise—it's a practical skill that enhances daily interactions. Whether you are leading a team, negotiating a deal, or nurturing personal relationships, the ability to read and respond appropriately to those around you can set the stage for mutual respect and understanding.

We've explored key concepts such as the significance of body language, the subtleties of facial expressions, and the critical role of tone and posture in communication. Each chapter is built upon the last, creating a comprehensive toolkit for real-world application.

To truly benefit from this book, I encourage you to practice regularly. Like any skill, proficiency in reading nonverbal cues comes from consistent effort and mindful observation. Start with small, manageable goals, such as noticing how people's expressions align with their spoken words or paying attention to your body language during conversations.

While this guide provides a robust foundation, it is not exhaustive. Human behavior is a vast and varied field, and much remains to be explored. Continued learning through additional reading, courses, or workshops can further enhance your understanding and skills.

Now is the time to take action. Use what you've learned to foster deeper connections with others, build stronger relationships, and move forward in your personal and professional life with greater assurance and empathy.

To leave you with a thought that encapsulates our shared journey:

"The most important thing in communication is

hearing what isn't said."

Peter Drucker

May this insight inspire you to listen with your ears, eyes, and heart.

Conclusion

"We have two ears and one mouth so that we

can listen twice as much as we speak."

Epictetus

As we reach the end of our exploration of nonverbal communication, it's essential to reflect on the journey we've undertaken. We've delved into the fundamental aspects of body language, facial expressions, and cultural nuances, which profoundly shape our interactions. Recognizing the power and influence of these silent signals can transform our personal and professional relationships, granting us a deeper connection with those around us.

Throughout this book, we have emphasized the importance of cultural sensitivity and awareness. Nonverbal cues can vary significantly across different cultures, and understanding these differences is crucial for effective cross-cultural communication. The ability to identify and respect these variations not only helps in avoiding misunderstandings but also fosters mutual respect and empathy, essential components of any meaningful relationship.

Emotional intelligence has emerged as a keystone in mastering nonverbal communication. We can manage interactions with greater finesse by heightening our awareness of our emotions and those of others. This book has provided practical strategies to enhance your emotional intelligence, helping you to respond more appropriately and effectively in various situations.

Practical application of the concepts discussed has been a consistent theme, highlighting the relevance of nonverbal communication skills in everyday life. Whether you're in a leadership role, negotiating a complex deal, or engaging in casual conversations, the techniques you've learned can be seamlessly integrated to improve the quality and clarity of your interactions.

Moreover, this book has underscored the importance of continuous learning. As human behavior is an ever-evolving field, staying curious and open to new insights will keep your skills sharp and relevant. The tools and strategies offered here serve as a solid foundation for building and refining your communication abilities over time.

Practical exercises and tips were provided to aid in your journey, emphasizing the need for consistent practice. Developing proficiency in nonverbal communication requires time and mindful observation. Start small, observe keenly, and gradually expand your practice to incorporate more nuanced cues and complex interactions.

In conclusion, reading and responding to nonverbal communication is a powerful asset. It's a skill that promotes deeper understanding and stronger connections, facilitating more effective and empathetic interactions. By embracing the techniques and insights shared in this book, you are better equipped to navigate the complexities of human interactions with confidence and grace.

To encapsulate the core takeaways:

- **Practice consistently:** Regularly observe and interpret nonverbal cues in different contexts.
- **Cultivate cultural sensitivity:** Be aware of and respect cultural differences in nonverbal communication.
- **Enhance emotional intelligence:** Develop a deeper awareness of your emotions and those of others.
- **Apply practically:** Use the skills learned to improve personal and professional interactions.
- **Engage in continuous learning:** Stay curious and open to new discoveries in nonverbal communication.
- **Start small:** Begin with manageable goals and gradually build your proficiency.

By integrating these principles into your daily life, you will find that authentic and effective communication becomes second nature. Embrace this ongoing journey and let your enhanced understanding of nonverbal cues enrich your relationships and interactions.

Bonus Material

Your Questions, Answered!

1. How can I apply the nonverbal communication techniques discussed in the book to virtual meetings?

Applying nonverbal communication techniques to virtual meetings may seem challenging at first, given the limitations of a digital environment. However, you can still effectively convey and interpret nonverbal cues through a screen with mindful practice and the right strategies. Start by ensuring your camera is positioned to capture your upper body, as gestures and body language are essential components of nonverbal communication. Maintain a good posture to project confidence and approachability. Additionally, cultivating a well-lit setup ensures your facial expressions are clearly visible, allowing others to read your emotions and reactions more accurately.

Active listening is another crucial aspect to consider. Even in virtual settings, showing that you are engaged and attentive involves affirming nods, maintaining appropriate eye contact by looking into the camera, and providing verbal acknowledgments like "I see" or "I understand." These subtle cues signal to others that their contributions are valued and respected. Don't underestimate the power of facial expressions; a genuine smile or a thoughtful frown can significantly enhance your communication and clarify your messages.

Moreover, knowing the potential for misinterpreting nonverbal cues in a virtual context is important. The lack of physical presence can sometimes lead to misunderstandings. For instance, a glance away from the screen might be interpreted as disinterest when you are just checking notes. To mitigate such misunderstandings, aim to be as explicit as possible in your verbal communication, supplementing nonverbal cues with clear, concise language. If you notice any ambiguity or confusion, don't hesitate to address it directly and clarify your intentions.

Finally, practice and feedback are key to improving virtual nonverbal communication skills. Record your meetings and review them to observe your body language and expressions. Identify areas for improvement, such as maintaining eye contact or ensuring your gestures are visible and purposeful. Seeking colleague feedback can also provide valuable insights and help you fine-tune your approach. By consistently refining these skills, you'll become more adept at conveying and interpreting nonverbal cues, making your virtual interactions more effective and engaging.

2. What are some common mistakes people make when interpreting body language?

Interpreting body language is intricate and rich with subtle cues and context-dependent signals. One common mistake is overgeneralizing specific gestures or expressions without considering the context. For instance, crossing arms might often be interpreted as a sign of defensiveness or closed-off behavior. However, in some cases, it could indicate that a person is cold or comfortable standing that way. Context is crucial, as the same gesture can convey different messages depending on the situation, environment, and individual differences.

Another prevalent mistake is projecting one's feelings or biases onto others when interpreting body language. This phenomenon, known as projection bias, can lead to misunderstandings and incorrect assumptions. For example, if someone feels anxious, they might misinterpret a colleague's neutral facial expression as disapproving or hostile. Being aware of one's emotional state and striving for objectivity can mitigate the inaccuracies caused by this bias. It's essential to consider the person's typical behavior and unique communication style to make a more accurate interpretation.

Additionally, overemphasizing isolated cues can distort the overall understanding of body language. Effective interpretation requires observing clusters of behaviors rather than single gestures. A fleeting frown, for example, might not hold much significance by itself. However, other signs, such as tense posture and minimal eye contact, can point toward discomfort or disagreement. Therefore, considering the congruency and patterns of multiple nonverbal cues provides a more holistic and accurate reading of a person's feelings and intentions.

Lastly, neglecting cultural differences is a significant pitfall in interpreting body language. Nonverbal communication is heavily influenced by cultural norms and practices, which can vary widely across different societies. A gesture or expression that is perfectly acceptable and clear in one culture may be misinterpreted in another. For instance, maintaining direct eye contact is generally seen as a sign of confidence in many Western cultures. In contrast, in some Asian cultures, it might be perceived as disrespectful or confrontational. Being culturally sensitive and informed can prevent such misunderstandings and enhance effective communication.

By recognizing these common errors and adopting a more nuanced, contextual, and culturally aware approach, one can significantly improve their ability to accurately interpret body language. This refined skill fosters better understanding, reduces miscommunication, and enhances interpersonal interactions across various settings.

3. How can I improve my ability to detect micro-expressions?

Improving your ability to detect micro-expressions involves understanding their significance, practicing observation, and developing emotional intelligence. Microexpressions are brief, involuntary facial expressions that last about half a second and reflect a person's true emotions. These fleeting expressions can reveal concealed feelings and provide invaluable insights into someone's emotional state, making them a powerful tool for enhancing communication and empathy.

To start, gaining theoretical knowledge about micro-expressions and their relevance is essential. Familiarize yourself with the seven universal emotions identified by psychologist Paul Ekman: happiness, sadness, surprise, fear, anger, disgust, and contempt. Each of these emotions has distinct micro-expressions that can be identified by specific facial movements. Utilizing resources such as books, online courses, and video tutorials on nonverbal communication can bolster your understanding and prepare you for real-world application.

Next, focused practice is crucial for honing this skill. Training exercises involving observing and interpreting micro-expressions can enhance your detection abilities. Online tools and apps like the Micro Expressions Training Tool (METT) and Subtle Expression Training Tool (SETT) offer interactive platforms for practicing and receiving feedback. These tools display various micro-expressions at different speeds, allowing you to progressively refine your ability to recognize them accurately and quickly.

Emotional intelligence also plays a significant role in detecting micro-expressions. Emotional awareness helps you empathize with others and perceive their emotions more accurately. Regular mindfulness and empathy exercises can elevate your emotional intelligence. For instance, practicing mindfulness meditation can heighten your awareness of subtle emotional cues, while engaging in active listening can deepen your understanding of others' feelings, thereby improving your ability to detect micro-expressions.

Moreover, analytical thinking can augment your ability to spot micro-expressions. Analyzing the context and other nonverbal signals is beneficial instead of jumping to conclusions based on an observed micro-expression. For example, if someone shows a brief flash of fear, consider the circumstances that might trigger such a reaction. Cross-referencing facial cues with body language, tone of voice, and situational factors provides a more comprehensive and accurate interpretation of the emotions at play.

By integrating these methods—acquiring knowledge, practicing regularly, developing emotional intelligence, and employing analytical thinking—you can significantly improve your ability to detect micro-expressions. This skill enhances interpersonal communication and empathy and equips you with a deeper understanding of human emotional dynamics.

4. In what ways can nonverbal communication influence my professional relationships?

Nonverbal communication significantly impacts professional relationships as it often complements or overrides verbal communication. The subtleties in facial expressions, gestures, posture, and eye contact can communicate confidence, empathy, and attentiveness—or, conversely, insecurity, indifference, and distraction. Mastering nonverbal cues can enhance your ability to establish rapport, build trust, and foster a positive work environment. For instance, maintaining appropriate eye contact can signal that you are actively listening and engaged, whereas crossing your arms might unintentionally convey defensiveness or resistance.

One of the key areas where nonverbal communication plays a crucial role is leadership. Effective leaders are adept at using body language to inspire and motivate their teams. Positive nonverbal cues, such as nodding in agreement, smiling, and maintaining an open posture, can create an atmosphere of encouragement and support, increasing team morale and productivity. Conversely, negative nonverbal signals, like frowning or avoiding eye contact, can diminish a leader's perceived confidence and approachability, potentially creating a barrier between them and their team members.

In addition to leadership, nonverbal communication is instrumental in the negotiation and conflict resolution. Reading the body language of others can provide insights into their true sentiments and openness to compromise. For example, noticing a counterpart's micro-expressions—such as flashes of surprise or doubt—can inform your negotiating strategy. Being attuned to these subtle cues allows you to adjust your approach dynamically, fostering a more collaborative and resolution-oriented dialogue.

Moreover, nonverbal communication is integral to networking

and relationship building. In professional settings, first impressions are often formed based on nonverbal cues before a word is spoken. A firm handshake, genuine smile, and confident posture can positively impact potential clients, partners, or employers. Similarly, being aware of cultural differences in nonverbal communication ensures that your gestures and expressions are appropriate and respectful, further solidifying strong international professional relationships.

Overall, being skilled in nonverbal communication is a powerful asset in the professional realm. It enhances your ability to convey empathy, assertiveness, and credibility, strengthening your interpersonal interactions and contributing to your career success. By focusing on and refining your nonverbal communication skills, you can navigate complex professional landscapes more effectively and establish meaningful and productive relationships.

5. How can cultural differences in nonverbal communication impact international business negotiations?

Cultural differences in nonverbal communication can significantly impact international business negotiations by facilitating understanding or creating misunderstandings. The interpretation of nonverbal cues such as gestures, facial expressions, proxemics (use of space), and eye contact varies widely across cultures. For example, in some cultures, maintaining direct eye contact is seen as a sign of confidence and honesty, while in others, it may be perceived as aggressive or disrespectful. Similarly, benign or positive gestures in one culture might be offensive in another. This divergence can lead to misinterpretations of intentions and sentiments, potentially causing friction and stalled negotiations.

Proxemics, or the acceptable physical distance during interactions, also vary among cultures and can influence the comfort level of the negotiating parties. Cultures with a high tolerance for physical closeness during conversations, such as those in Latin America or the Middle East, might find it off-putting if their counterparts from cultures that value personal space, such as in North America or Northern Europe, seem to keep their distance. This difference in personal space expectations can create an unintended impression of aloofness or disinterest, hindering the development of trust and rapport necessary for successful negotiations.

Moreover, the use and meaning of nonverbal signals, like hand gestures, can differ dramatically across cultural lines. For instance, the thumbs-up gesture is a common sign of approval in many Western cultures. Still, it can be considered rude or offensive in parts of the Middle East. Similarly, nodding or shaking the head can mean different things in different cultures; what is universally understood as a nod for agreement may signal the opposite in certain contexts. Such discrepancies necessitate a keen cultural awareness and sensitivity to avoid miscommunications that could derail the negotiation process.

Facial expressions also play a critical role and can be misinterpreted if cultural nuances are not understood. In some Asian cultures, for instance, showing too much emotion through facial expressions can be perceived as a lack of control. In contrast, Western cultures might interpret the same as being open and sincere. Understanding these subtle differences can prevent misjudgments and foster a more harmonious negotiating environment.

To mitigate these potential challenges, negotiators must invest time in understanding the cultural backgrounds of their international counterparts. This involves learning about specific nonverbal communication norms and being observant and adaptive during interactions. Employing a cross-cultural consultant or participating in cultural sensitivity training can significantly enhance negotiators' competencies in this area. By acknowledging and respecting these cultural differences, negotiators can improve their ability to forge stronger, more effective international business relationships.

6. What are some effective exercises to practice emotional intelligence in everyday situations?

Practicing emotional intelligence in everyday situations is crucial for personal and professional growth. One effective strategy is through mindfulness meditation. Mindfulness helps individuals develop a deeper awareness of their emotions and reactions, allowing them to respond thoughtfully rather than impulsively. Setting aside just a few minutes each day to focus on the present moment can cultivate a greater sense of calm and clarity, ultimately enhancing your emotional regulation. This practice enables you to acknowledge and understand your emotions, fostering greater empathy and better management of interpersonal relationships.

Another valuable exercise involves active listening. Active listening is more than just hearing words; it requires fully concentrating, understanding, and responding thoughtfully to what is being said. To practice this, engage in conversations without interrupting or planning your response while the other person is speaking. Instead, focus on their words, tone, and body language. Summarize what you have heard and ask clarifying questions if needed. This improves listening skills, shows respect, and validates the other person's feelings and viewpoints, promoting stronger, more empathetic relationships.

Journaling is also an effective way to enhance emotional intelligence. By writing down your thoughts and feelings, you can reflect on your reactions to various scenarios and identify patterns in your emotional responses. This practice can help you better understand the triggers that influence your emotions and develop strategies to manage them more effectively. Additionally, journaling allows you to track your progress over time, providing tangible evidence of your emotional awareness and regulation growth.

Another exercise to practice emotional intelligence is role-playing different scenarios that could arise in your daily life. This can be particularly beneficial in a professional setting where difficult conversations or conflicts occur. You can experiment with different responses and strategies in a safe environment by simulating these situations with a trusted friend or mentor. This helps build confidence and prepares you to handle real-life interactions with greater emotional control and empathy.

Lastly, seeking feedback from others on your emotional intelligence can provide valuable insights into areas where you excel and areas that need improvement. Encourage colleagues, friends, or family members to offer constructive criticism about your emotional interactions. Use this feedback to reflect on your behavior and consciously adjust accordingly. Being open to feedback and continuously working on your emotional skills can significantly enhance your emotional intelligence, leading to more fulfilling and effective relationships in all aspects of your life.

7. How do nonverbal cues differ between genders, and how can I be more aware of these differences?

Nonverbal communication is critical to our daily interactions, yet it often goes unnoticed. Recognizing how nonverbal cues differ between genders can substantially enhance our understanding and improve our interpersonal relationships. Men and women tend to express themselves differently through body language, facial expressions, and tone of voice, which can lead to misunderstandings if not properly interpreted. For instance, research has shown that women are generally more expressive than men regarding nonverbal signals, often using more facial expressions, gestures, and eye contact to convey their emotions. This expressiveness can sometimes be perceived as more open and communicative.

Conversely, men may rely more on physical space and gestural economy, often using fewer but more pronounced gestures. They might exhibit dominance-oriented nonverbal cues, such as postural expansiveness or interrupting more frequently. These differences can be traced to varied socialization patterns where men typically learn to exhibit more assertive and less emotionally revealing behaviors. Understanding these tendencies can help interpret nonverbal cues more accurately, enabling better communication.

One can start by observing people in various social and professional settings to be more aware of these differences. Notice how men and women use their bodies, faces, and voices to express themselves. Pay attention to the context in which these nonverbal behaviors occur, as they can vary significantly depending on the situation. For instance, catching slight changes in posture, eye movements, or hand gestures during a business meeting versus a social gathering can provide valuable insights.

Additionally, seeking educational resources on nonverbal communication and gender can expand your knowledge. Books, workshops, and online courses can offer in-depth exploration and practical tips. Understanding cultural nuances is also crucial, as how genders use nonverbal cues can differ across cultures. Engaging in discussions and seeking feedback from peers or mentors can also help refine your awareness, as they might offer perspectives you haven't considered.

Adopting a sensitive and observant approach can make one more adept at reading and interpreting gender-specific nonverbal cues. This fosters more effective communication and leads to stronger, more empathetic, and authentic relationships in both personal and professional spheres.

8. Can nonverbal communication help in conflict resolution? If so, how?

Nonverbal communication plays a vital role in conflict resolution, often serving as a complement to verbal interactions. In many cases, what is left unsaid can significantly influence the direction of a discussion or negotiation. Nonverbal cues such as facial expressions, body posture, gestures, and eye contact can convey empathy, attentiveness, and a willingness to understand, which are all crucial for resolving conflicts. By being aware of and deliberately using nonverbal signals, individuals can create a more conducive environment for open and honest dialogue, facilitating a more amicable resolution.

One way nonverbal communication aids in conflict resolution is by demonstrating active listening. When someone nods their head, maintains eye contact, and leans in slightly, these actions indicate that they are engaged and taking the other's viewpoint seriously. This can help to de-escalate tension and make the other party feel heard and valued. Such nonverbal affirmations build a sense of mutual respect and trust, which is foundational for resolving disagreements.

Another powerful aspect of nonverbal communication in conflict resolution is the ability to express emotions without words. For example, a calm demeanor can help soothe an agitated party. At the same time, a warm smile or reassuring touch can diffuse anger and promote a more cooperative atmosphere. Conversely, aggressive nonverbal cues like crossed arms, rolling eyes, or a frown can exacerbate the situation, making resolution more difficult. Therefore, understanding how to control and employ nonverbal signals can be pivotal in navigating conflicts effectively.

Moreover, recognizing and interpreting the nonverbal cues of others can provide insights into their emotional state and underlying concerns that may not be explicitly stated. For instance, noticing someone avoiding eye contact, fidgeting, or displaying discomfort can prompt inquiries that help uncover hidden issues or frustrations. Addressing these unarticulated concerns can lead to a more comprehensive and satisfactory resolution.

In conclusion, nonverbal communication is an essential tool for conflict resolution. It supports verbal communication by reinforcing messages, demonstrating empathy, and creating a respectful and understanding atmosphere. By honing skills in observing and utilizing nonverbal cues, individuals can navigate conflicts more effectively, leading to stronger and more resilient relationships.

9. How can I tell if someone is being deceitful based on their body language?

Detecting deceit through body language involves observing various nonverbal cues that might indicate dishonesty or discomfort. While no single gesture or expression offers definitive proof of deceit, a combination of several signals can suggest that someone is not being entirely truthful. These signs often arise from the cognitive load and emotional stress that lying imposes on an individual.

One classic indicator of deceit is inconsistency between verbal and nonverbal communication. For instance, if someone says they are confident. Still, their body language shows closed posture, such as crossed arms or legs, which may signal underlying unease. Similarly, micro-expressions—brief, involuntary facial expressions—can reveal true emotions that contradict spoken words. These fleeting expressions are often too quick to control and can provide valuable insights into a person's feelings.

Another key sign to monitor is eye behavior. While common myths suggest that liars avoid eye contact, the reality is more complex. Some deceptive individuals may overcompensate by maintaining unnaturally prolonged eye contact to appear sincere. However, frequent blinking, pupil dilation, and rapid changes in gaze or avoiding eye contact during critical moments can still indicate deceit. These eye movements can reflect the cognitive effort required to maintain a lie and simultaneously monitor the listener's reaction.

Physical gestures also offer clues. Lying people might display unusual or excessive body movements, such as fidgeting, touching their faces, or scratching their necks. These actions can be self-soothing mechanisms to cope with the anxiety of lying. Inconsistent gestures, such as shaking the head while affirming "yes," can also hint at dishonesty. Also, liars often use fewer gestures when speaking, possibly because they focus their mental resources on maintaining the deception.

Lastly, shifts in vocal tone and speech patterns can betray deceit. Watch for changes in pitch, speed, and hesitancy in speech. A person may suddenly start speaking faster or slower, have more pauses, or stumble over their words when they are not being truthful. The stress of lying can also affect voice pitch, causing it to rise. Paying attention to these verbal inconsistencies alongside body language cues can help form a more accurate assessment of whether someone is being deceitful.

Understanding and interpreting these nonverbal signals requires practice and context. While body language can provide significant insights, it should be considered alongside other information to draw reliable conclusions about someone's honesty.

10.   What role does personal space play in nonverbal communication, and how can I navigate it effectively?

Personal space, the physical distance we maintain between ourselves and others, is critical to nonverbal communication. It signifies boundaries and comfort levels, with variations influenced by cultural norms, relationships, and individual preferences. Understanding and respecting personal space can enhance interpersonal interactions, promoting safety, respect, and trust.

Different cultures have distinct norms regarding personal space. In some cultures, close physical proximity during conversations is typical and even expected, whereas, in others, greater distances are maintained to ensure comfort and respect. For instance, Mediterranean and Latin American cultures may stand closer to one another. In contrast, individuals from Northern European and East Asian cultures typically prefer more personal space. Being aware of these cultural differences can prevent misunderstandings and demonstrate cultural sensitivity.

Personal space varies not only by culture but also by the nature of relationships. Intimate zones are reserved for close relationships like family members and friends. At the same time, personal and social distances are maintained between acquaintances and strangers. Navigating these distances effectively requires situational awareness and adaptability. For example, standing too close during a professional meeting may be perceived as intrusive, while maintaining too much distance in a friendly gathering could seem aloof or disengaged.

Effective navigation of personal space involves keen observation and responsiveness to nonverbal cues. If someone steps back or turns slightly away, it may signal that they need more space. Conversely, leaning in or stepping closer can indicate comfort and interest. Mirroring the other person's body language and maintaining an appropriate distance shows attentiveness and respect for their boundaries. Additionally, using open body language and avoiding barriers, such as crossed arms or objects in between, can enhance connection and communication.

In conclusion, personal space is pivotal in nonverbal communication, influencing how messages are received and interpreted. By understanding cultural norms, relationship dynamics, and nonverbal signals, individuals can navigate personal space effectively, fostering positive and respectful interactions. These skills can enhance personal and professional relationships, leading to more meaningful and successful communications.

11. How can understanding nonverbal communication improve my leadership skills?

Understanding nonverbal communication is crucial for effective leadership, as it encompasses how people convey messages without words, such as through facial expressions, body language, gestures, posture, and eye contact. Leaders adept at interpreting these nonverbal cues possess a valuable skill that can enhance their ability to connect with team members, foster trust, and create a positive work environment. By being attuned to the subtleties of nonverbal communication, leaders can better understand their team's emotions and reactions, allowing them to address concerns proactively and empathetically.

First, nonverbal communication can significantly impact how a leader perceives and understands messages. Effective leaders use positive body language, such as maintaining an open posture, eye contact, and appropriate gestures, to convey confidence, approachability, and clarity. These nonverbal signals can reinforce verbal messages, making them more persuasive and compelling. Additionally, leaders aware of their nonverbal cues can avoid sending mixed messages that might confuse or demotivate their team.

Secondly, understanding nonverbal communication enables leaders to detect unspoken issues within the team. Employees might hesitate to voice their concerns directly. Still, they may exhibit signs of discomfort, stress, or dissatisfaction through their body language. For instance, frequent fidgeting, avoiding eye contact, or closed postures could indicate an employee feeling uneasy or unengaged. By recognizing these signals, a leader can initiate open and supportive conversations to address underlying issues, fostering a more transparent and trusting work environment.

Moreover, nonverbal communication skills enhance a leader's ability to build rapport and strong relationships with team members. When leaders show empathy and attentiveness through nonverbal behaviors, such as nodding in agreement, mirroring gestures, or reassuring smiles, they create a sense of connection and mutual respect. This approach not only boosts team morale but also encourages collaboration and loyalty. Team members are more likely to feel valued and understood when their leader actively listens and responds to verbal and nonverbal cues.

Lastly, effective interpretation of nonverbal communication can aid in conflict resolution and negotiation. During tense interactions, a leader who is sensitive to the nonverbal signals of others can better gauge emotions and adjust their approach accordingly. For instance, recognizing when someone is becoming defensive or agitated allows the leader to de-escalate the situation, perhaps by adopting a calmer tone or conciliatory gesture. This ability to read and respond appropriately to nonverbal cues can lead to more successful resolution of conflicts and more productive negotiations.

In summary, understanding nonverbal communication is a pivotal component of impactful leadership. It enhances message delivery, helps identify unspoken issues, strengthens relationships, and improves conflict management. Leaders who master nonverbal communication can foster a supportive and dynamic team environment, driving individual and organizational success.

12. What strategies can I use to become more observant of nonverbal cues during conversations?

Becoming more observant of nonverbal cues during conversations involves developing a heightened awareness of the signals people send through their body language, facial expressions, and other nonverbal behaviors. One effective strategy is practicing active listening, not merely hearing the words spoken. This involves fully concentrating, understanding, responding, and then remembering what is being said while paying attention to the speaker's nonverbal signals. By focusing on the speaker's tone of voice, eye contact, and gestures, you can better understand their emotional state and intent. Active listening also involves providing engagement and empathy feedback, such as nodding or maintaining appropriate eye contact.

Another useful strategy is enhancing observational skills through consistent practice and mindfulness. Start by setting aside a few minutes each day to observe people in various settings, such as meetings, social gatherings, or public places. Take note of their body language, facial expressions, and movements without judging or interpreting them immediately. This practice helps you become more attuned to subtle nonverbal cues. In conversations, make a conscious effort to scan the person's body language periodically. Look for congruence between their words and actions, as discrepancies can often indicate underlying emotions or thoughts that are not verbally expressed.

Understanding cultural differences in nonverbal communication is also crucial. Nonverbal behaviors can vary widely across cultural contexts, and misinterpreting these cues can lead to misunderstandings. Research and educate yourself about the cultural norms of the people you interact with frequently. This knowledge can help you interpret nonverbal signals more accurately and respond in a manner that is respectful and appropriate. For instance, while maintaining eye contact might be a sign of confidence in some cultures, it could be considered disrespectful in others. Being culturally aware ensures that you navigate nonverbal communication with sensitivity and precision.

Engaging in role-playing exercises or attending workshops on nonverbal communication can further enhance your ability to observe and interpret these cues. Role-playing provides a safe environment to practice reading and using nonverbal signals effectively. It allows you to receive immediate feedback and make adjustments in real-time. On the other hand, workshops offer structured learning experiences guided by experts who can provide insights and techniques for observing nonverbal cues. These educational opportunities can significantly boost your confidence and proficiency in nonverbal communication.

In conclusion, becoming more observant of nonverbal cues during conversations requires active listening, consistent practice, cultural awareness, and educational experiences like role-playing and workshops. Developing these strategies can improve your ability to connect with others, foster empathy, and enhance your overall communication skills. This heightened awareness and understanding of nonverbal behavior can lead to more meaningful and effective interactions in both personal and professional contexts.

13. Are there any nonverbal communication cues that remain consistent across different cultures?

While nonverbal communication can vary significantly across cultural contexts, certain cues are universally recognized and understood. One such example is facial expressions related to basic human emotions. Research in psychology, particularly the work of Dr. Paul Ekman, has shown that expressions of emotions like happiness, sadness, anger, and fear are largely consistent across diverse cultures. For instance, a smile is generally seen as an indicator of happiness. At the same time, a frown is commonly associated with sadness or displeasure. These universal facial expressions are fundamental to human nonverbal communication, transcending cultural boundaries and language differences.

Another consistent nonverbal cue involves body language related to openness or defensiveness. Across cultures, an open posture—such as uncrossed arms and legs and maintaining an upright, welcoming stance—typically signals receptiveness and attentiveness. Conversely, a closed posture, characterized by crossed arms and legs or turning the body away from the speaker, generally indicates discomfort or defensive feelings. These physical markers of emotional states are often instinctive and deeply rooted in human behavior, making them relatively consistent worldwide.

Touch, or haptic communication, also contains some universal elements, although it is more nuanced due to cultural variations. A handshake, for example, is widely accepted as a formal greeting in many cultures, symbolizing politeness and mutual respect. While the specifics of the handshake—such as the duration, grip strength, and frequency—may differ, the fundamental concept remains analogous across numerous societies. Comforting gestures like a pat on the back or a hug often convey similar meanings of support and warmth. However, the appropriateness of these actions can depend on the context and the relationship between the individuals involved.

Eye contact is another nonverbal cue that holds some universal significance despite cultural differences in interpretation. Generally, eye contact is associated with attentiveness, interest, and sincerity. While the duration and intensity of eye contact can vary—being seen as respectful in some cultures and invasive in others—the underlying principle of using eye movements to convey engagement and honesty is largely recognized. A lack of eye contact may often be interpreted as disinterest or evasiveness, highlighting its essential role in effective communication.

While many nonverbal cues are subject to cultural interpretation and context, some fundamental aspects of body language, facial expressions, touch, and eye contact exhibit a universality. Understanding these consistent cues can enhance cross-cultural communication by helping individuals recognize and interpret basic emotional states and intentions, thus fostering clearer and more empathetic interactions.

14. How can I balance verbal and nonverbal communication to enhance my communication skills?

Balancing verbal and nonverbal communication effectively requires an understanding that these two forms of interaction complement each other. Verbal communication includes the words we use and the structure of those words to convey our thoughts. Nonverbal communication includes body language, facial expressions, gestures, and tone of voice. A harmonious balance between these elements can significantly enhance overall communication skills, making interactions more meaningful and effective.

To start, being mindful of consistency between verbal and nonverbal cues is essential. Inconsistencies can lead to confusion and mistrust. For instance, if you verbally express enthusiasm about a project, but your body language is closed off, and your tone is flat, the listener may doubt your sincerity. Ensuring your nonverbal cues reinforce your verbal messages can help build trustful and coherent communication. This congruence also reinforces the message, making it clearer and more impactful.

Additionally, active listening is critical in balancing verbal and nonverbal communication. Active listening involves hearing the words and observing the speaker's nonverbal cues. This includes maintaining eye contact, nodding, and responding with appropriate facial expressions and gestures that show attention and understanding. Doing so demonstrates your engagement and empathy, which enriches the conversation and fosters a stronger connection with the speaker.

Moreover, developing emotional intelligence can significantly aid in balancing these forms of communication. Emotional intelligence involves being aware of and managing your emotions while being sensitive to others' emotions through their verbal and nonverbal signals. Recognizing when someone's body language shifts or vocal tone changes allows you to adjust your communication style accordingly. This adaptability makes the interaction smoother and ensures that you address the other person's needs and feelings rather than just responding to their words.

Finally, practice and feedback are keys to mastering the balance between verbal and nonverbal communication. Engaging in regular role-playing exercises or communication workshops can provide a safe space to practice integrating these skills. Feedback from others can offer valuable insights into areas that need improvement. Over time, with consistent practice and constructive feedback, balancing verbal and nonverbal communication will become more natural, ultimately enhancing your overall communication proficiency.

15. What signs indicate someone is not engaged in a conversation, and how can I address it?

Recognizing signs of disengagement in a conversation is crucial for any meaningful interaction. Common disengagement indicators include lack of eye contact, distracted body language, and minimal verbal responses. For instance, if the person you are speaking to frequently looks away, their gaze is unfocused, or they consistently check their phone or watch, these could be clear signals of disinterest or distraction. Additionally, closed-off body language such as crossed arms or legs, leaning away from the speaker, or lack of responsive facial expressions may suggest they are not fully engaged in the conversation.

Addressing disengagement effectively requires a combination of verbal and nonverbal strategies. One immediate step is to pause and refocus the conversation. Gently asking if the timing is right for the discussion or if they have other concerns can provide an opening for addressing distractions. Sometimes, simply acknowledging that they seem distracted and asking how they feel can re-engage them by showing empathy and concern. This brings their attention back to the conversation and fosters a sense of mutual respect and understanding.

Another approach involves active engagement techniques. Open-ended questions related to their interests or opinions can stimulate their involvement in the conversation. By steering the discussion towards more relevant or interesting topics, you increase the chances of rekindling their attention. Additionally, using names throughout the conversation can help personalize the interaction and make the other person feel more valued and involved. This simple tactic can make a significant impact on their level of engagement.

Nonverbal adjustments can also play a key role in addressing disengagement. Mirroring the other person's body language subtly can create a subconscious bond, making them feel understood and connected. Maintaining eye contact, nodding, and using expressive facial gestures can signal interest and encourage reciprocation. Ensuring an open and approachable posture can invite the other person to re-engage. These small but powerful nonverbal cues often reignite a dwindling conversation by conveying attentiveness and interest.

In conclusion, identifying and addressing signs of disengagement requires a mindful approach that integrates verbal and nonverbal strategies. By creating a responsive and empathetic communication environment, you can effectively foster engagement and ensure it remains.

Thank You

Thank you for taking the time to read this book. Your dedication to improving your communication skills is truly commendable. We hope the insights and strategies provided will serve as valuable tools in enhancing your personal and professional interactions.

Remember, effective communication is a journey, and your commitment to learning is a significant step forward. Keep striving for clarity, empathy, and connection in all your conversations. Your efforts today will undoubtedly lead to richer, more meaningful relationships tomorrow.

Made in the USA
Monee, IL
13 January 2025